GERMAN
FOR EVERYONE
JUNIOR
5 WORDS A DAY

FREE AUDIO
website and app

www.dk5words.com/us

GERMAN
FOR EVERYONE
JUNIOR

5 WORDS A DAY

FREE AUDIO
website and app

www.dk5words.com/us

DK
For the curious

DK LONDON
Project Editors Sophie Adam, Elizabeth Blakemore
Project Art Editor Anna Scully
Designer Annabel Schick
Illustrators Amy Child, Gus Scott
Managing Editor Christine Stroyan
Managing Art Editor Anna Hall
Production Editor Kavita Varma
Production Controller Samantha Cross
Senior Jacket Designer Suhita Dharamjit
Jacket Design Development Manager Sophia MTT
Publisher Andrew Macintyre
Art Director Karen Self
Publishing Director Jonathan Metcalf

Translation Andiamo! Language Services Ltd

DK INDIA
Pre-Production Manager Sunil Sharma
DTP Designers Manish Chandra Upreti,
Umesh Singh Rawat

First American Edition, 2021
Published in the United States by DK Publishing
1450 Broadway, Suite 801, New York, NY 10018

A catalog record for this book
is available from the Library of Congress.
ISBN: 978-0-7440-3680-0
DK books are available at special discounts
when purchased in bulk for sales promotions, premiums,
fund-raising, or educational use. For details, contact:
DK Publishing Special Markets,
1450 Broadway, Suite 801, New York, NY 10018
SpecialSales@dk.com

Printed and bound in China

For the curious

www.dk.com

This book was made with Forest
Stewardship Council ™ certified
paper – one small step in DK's
commitment to a sustainable future.
For more information go to
www.dk.com/our-green-pledge

Contents

How to use this book   6

Week 1	8		Week 13	56
Week 2	12		Week 14	60
Week 3	16		Week 15	64
Week 4	20		Week 16	68
Week 5	24		Week 17	72
Week 6	28		Week 18	76
Week 7	32		Week 19	80
Week 8	36		Week 20	84
Week 9	40		Week 21	88
Week 10	44		Week 22	92
Week 11	48		Week 23	96
Week 12	52		Week 24	100

Max   Maria

Week 25	104	Week 37	152	Week 49	200
Week 26	108	Week 38	156	Week 50	204
Week 27	112	Week 39	160	Week 51	208
Week 28	116	Week 40	164	Week 52	212
Week 29	120	Week 41	168	Numbers	216
Week 30	124	Week 42	172	Days and months	217
Week 31	128	Week 43	176	English word list	218
Week 32	132	Week 44	180	German word list	224
Week 33	136	Week 45	184	Common subjects	231
Week 34	140	Week 46	188	Answers	232
Week 35	144	Week 47	192	Acknowledgments	240
Week 36	148	Week 48	196		

How to use this book

German for Everyone Junior: 5 Words a Day is a vocabulary book for children that teaches and tests more than 1,000 German words. Words are taught in weekly units of 5 days.

Learning new vocabulary

On Days 1–4, the child will be presented with 20 new words, which are taught 5 words at a time through colorful illustrations.

1 First, listen to the words on the audio app or website, repeat the words out loud, and then write them out in the space below each word.

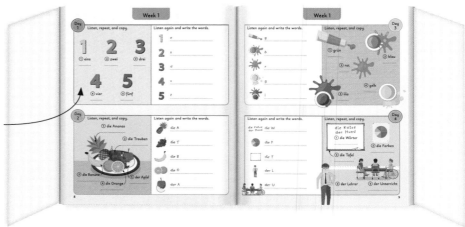

Masculine, feminine, and neuter words

In German, all nouns (things or people) are masculine, feminine, or neuter. You will notice that many words have "der", "das", or "die" in front of them. These all mean "the" in English. If a word has "der" before it, it is masculine. Words that appear after "die" are feminine or plural, and words that appear after "das" are neuter.

2 Next, use the book flaps to cover the illustrations and listen to the words again.

3 With the words still covered, try writing out each word from memory.

Testing new vocabulary

On Day 5, the child can practice the 20 new words and reinforce their learning through fun exercises.

A variety of exercises are used to test all 20 words.

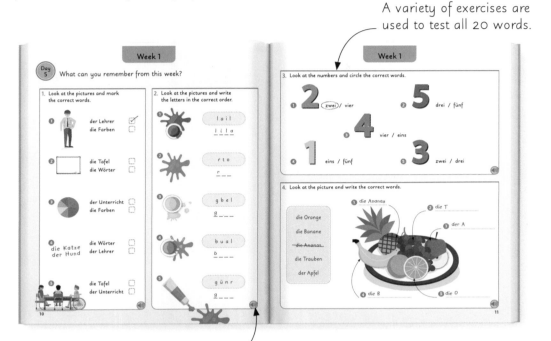

Once you have finished an exercise, listen to the words again on the app or website.

Answers to all the questions are given at the back of the book.

Audio

Pronunciation is an important aspect of learning a new language. Audio for all the words in this book is available on the **DK 5 Words** website and app. You should encourage your child to listen to the audio and repeat the words out loud.

Access the audio recordings for free at **www.dk5words.com/us** or download the **DK 5 Words** app from the App Store or Google Play.

FREE AUDIO
website and app

www.dk5words.com/us

Day 1

Listen, repeat, and copy.

1 ① eins

2 ② zwei

3 ③ drei

4 ④ vier

5 ⑤ fünf

Listen again and write the words.

1 e

2 z

3 d

4 v

5 f

Day 2

Listen, repeat, and copy.

① die Ananas

② die Trauben

③ die Banane

④ die Orange

⑤ der Apfel

Listen again and write the words.

die A

die T

die B

die O

der A

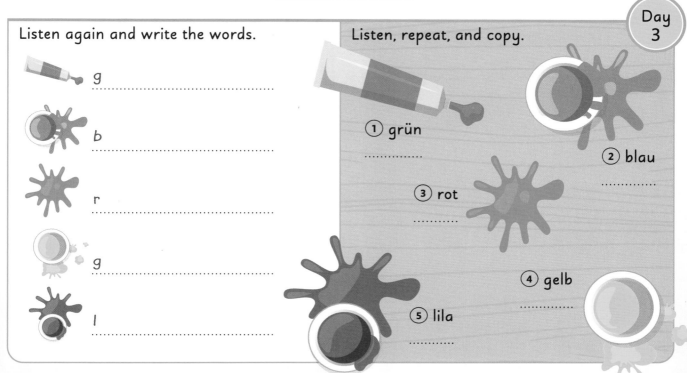

Day 3

Listen again and write the words.

g ....

b ....

r ....

g ....

l ....

Listen, repeat, and copy.

① grün
....

② blau
....

③ rot
....

④ gelb
....

⑤ lila
....

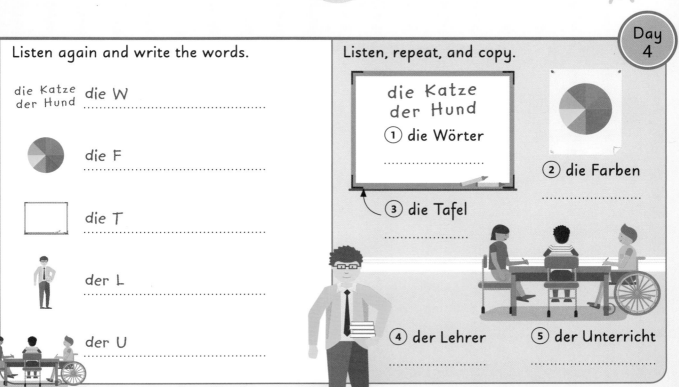

Day 4

Listen again and write the words.

die Katze
der Hund → die W ....

die F ....

die T ....

der L ....

der U ....

Listen, repeat, and copy.

die Katze
der Hund
① die Wörter
....

② die Farben
....

③ die Tafel
....

④ der Lehrer
....

⑤ der Unterricht
....

What can you remember from this week?

1. Look at the pictures and mark the correct words.

1. der Lehrer ☑
   die Farben ☐

2. die Tafel ☐
   die Wörter ☐

3. der Unterricht ☐
   die Farben ☐

4. die Wörter ☐
   der Lehrer ☐

5. die Tafel ☐
   der Unterricht ☐

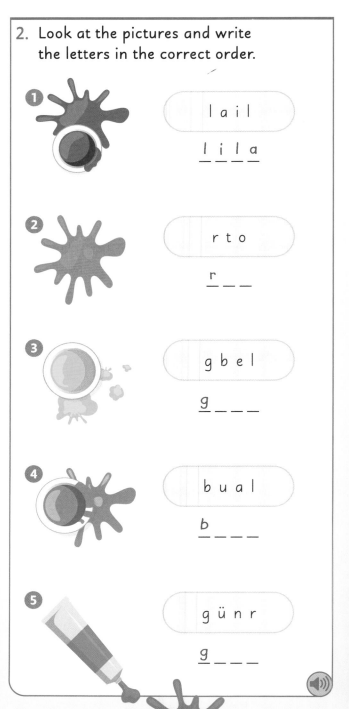

2. Look at the pictures and write the letters in the correct order.

1. l a i l
   l i l a
   _ _ _ _

2. r t o
   r _ _ _

3. g b e l
   g _ _ _ _

4. b u a l
   b _ _ _ _

5. g ü n r
   g _ _ _ _

3. Look at the numbers and circle the correct words.

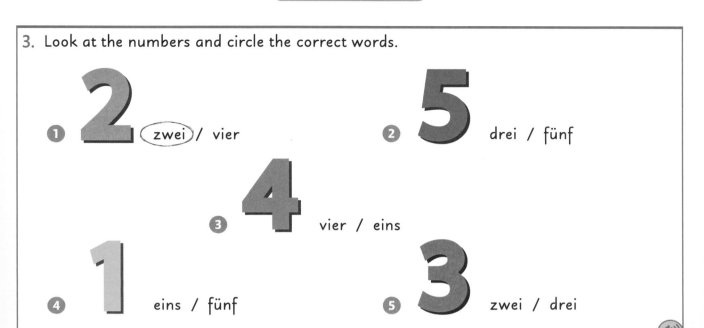

① **2** (zwei) / vier

② **5** drei / fünf

③ **4** vier / eins

④ **1** eins / fünf

⑤ **3** zwei / drei

4. Look at the picture and write the correct words.

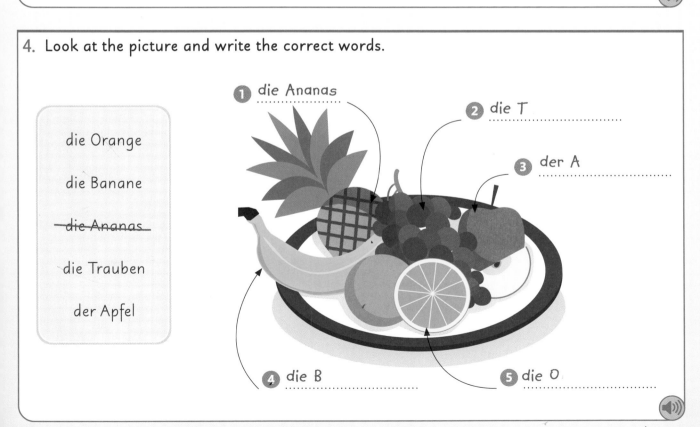

die Orange

die Banane

~~die Ananas~~

die Trauben

der Apfel

① die Ananas

② die T ....

③ der A ....

④ die B ....

⑤ die O ....

Day 1

Listen, repeat, and copy.

6 ① sechs

7 ② sieben

8 ③ acht

9 ④ neun

10 ⑤ zehn

Listen again and write the words.

6 s ....

7 s ....

8 a ....

9 n ....

10 z ....

Day 2

Listen, repeat, and copy.

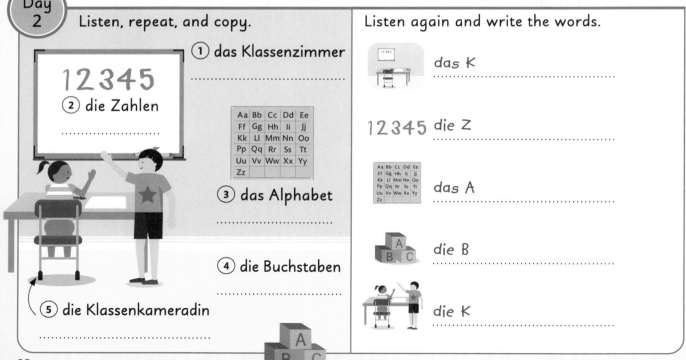

① das Klassenzimmer

12345
② die Zahlen

Aa	Bb	Cc	Dd	Ee
Ff	Gg	Hh	Ii	Jj
Kk	Ll	Mm	Nn	Oo
Pp	Qq	Rr	Ss	Tt
Uu	Vv	Ww	Xx	Yy
Zz				

③ das Alphabet

④ die Buchstaben

⑤ die Klassenkameradin

Listen again and write the words.

das K ....

12345 die Z ....

das A ....

die B ....

die K ....

Week 2

Listen again and write the words.

die M ....

die A ....

der T ....

das B ....

die P ....

Listen, repeat, and copy.

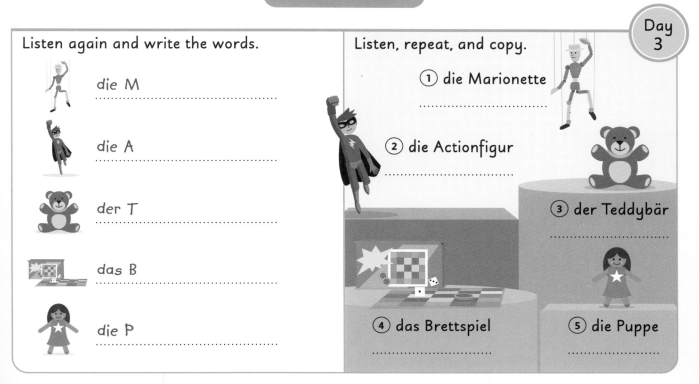

① die Marionette
....

② die Actionfigur
....

③ der Teddybär
....

④ das Brettspiel
....

⑤ die Puppe
....

Listen again and write the words.

der K ....

die F ....

der B ....

die W ....

das P ....

Listen, repeat, and copy.

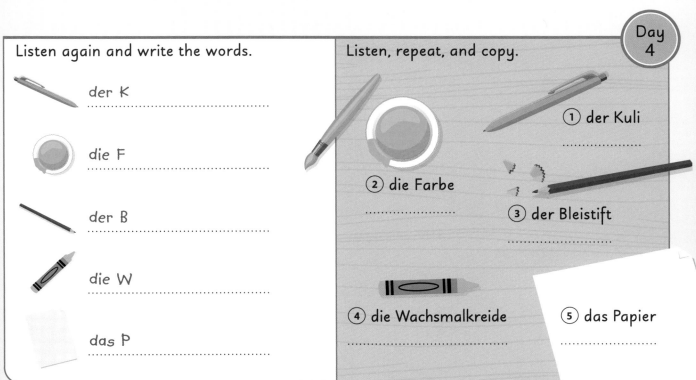

① der Kuli
....

② die Farbe
....

③ der Bleistift
....

④ die Wachsmalkreide
....

⑤ das Papier
....

Day 5

What can you remember from this week?

1. Look at the pictures and write the correct words.

das Alphabet   ~~die Zahlen~~   die Klassenkameradin
die Buchstaben   das Klassenzimmer

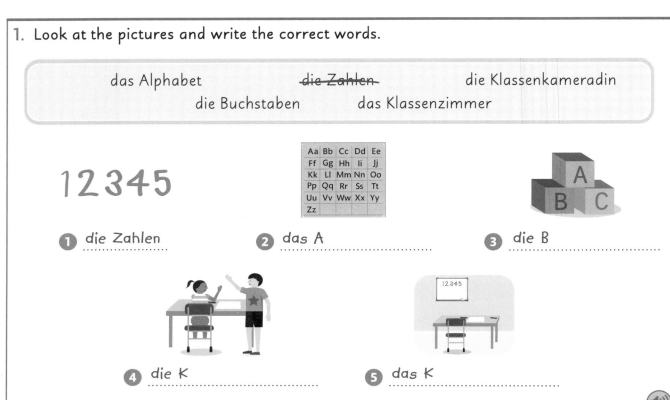

① die Zahlen

② das A

③ die B

④ die K

⑤ das K

2. Match the pictures to the correct words.

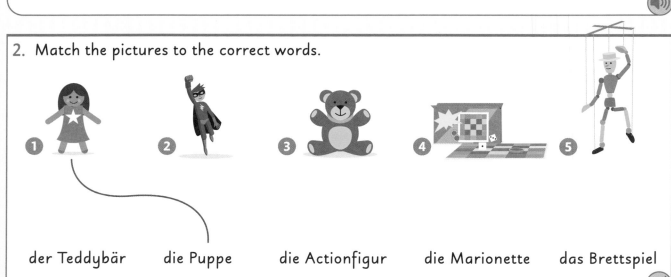

der Teddybär   die Puppe   die Actionfigur   die Marionette   das Brettspiel

3. Read the words and mark the correct pictures.

1 der Kuli   A ☐   B ☑

2 die Wachsmalkreide   A ☐   B ☐

3 das Papier   A ☐   B ☐

4 die Farbe   A ☐   B ☐

5 der Bleistift   A ☐   B ☐

4. Look at the numbers and fill in the missing letters.

1 **8**   a c h t

2 **6**   _ e _ h _

3 **9**   n _ _ u _

4 **7**   _ _ _ i _ b _ n

5 **10**   z _ h _

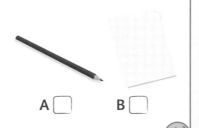

Day 1

Listen, repeat, and copy.

11 ① elf

....

12 ② zwölf

....

13 ③ dreizehn

....

14 ④ vierzehn

....

15 ⑤ fünfzehn

....

Listen again and write the words.

11 e ....

12 z ....

13 d ....

14 v ....

15 f ....

Day 2

Listen, repeat, and copy.

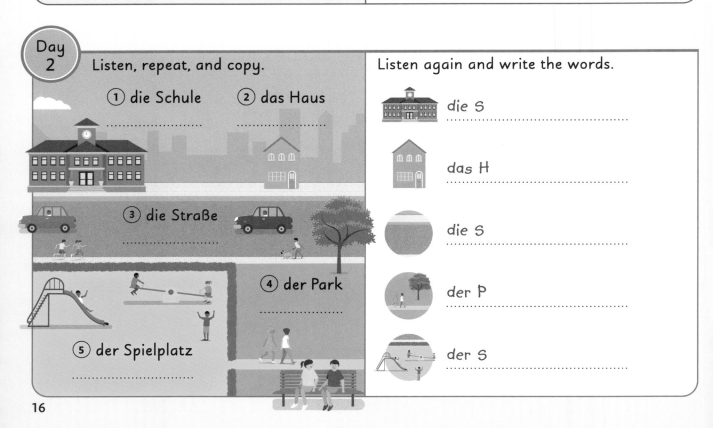

① die Schule

② das Haus

③ die Straße

....

④ der Park

....

⑤ der Spielplatz

....

Listen again and write the words.

die S ....

das H ....

die S ....

der P ....

der S ....

Week 3

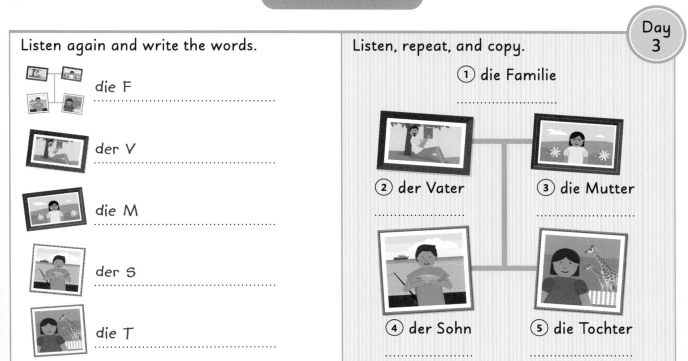

Day 3

Listen again and write the words.

die F ....

der V ....

die M ....

der S ....

die T ....

Listen, repeat, and copy.

① die Familie

....

② der Vater   ③ die Mutter

....

④ der Sohn   ⑤ die Tochter

....

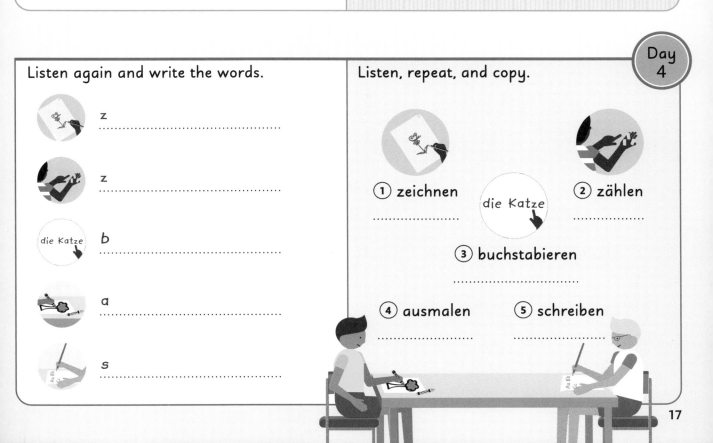

Day 4

Listen again and write the words.

z ....

z ....

b ....

a ....

s ....

Listen, repeat, and copy.

① zeichnen   die Katze   ② zählen

....

③ buchstabieren

....

④ ausmalen   ⑤ schreiben

....

17

Day 5

What can you remember from this week?

1. Look at the pictures and mark the correct words.

① zeichnen ✓
   buchstabieren ☐

② ausmalen ☐
   zählen ☐

③ zählen ☐
   schreiben ☐

④ *die Katze*
   ausmalen ☐
   buchstabieren ☐

⑤ zeichnen ☐
   schreiben ☐

2. Match the pictures to the correct words.

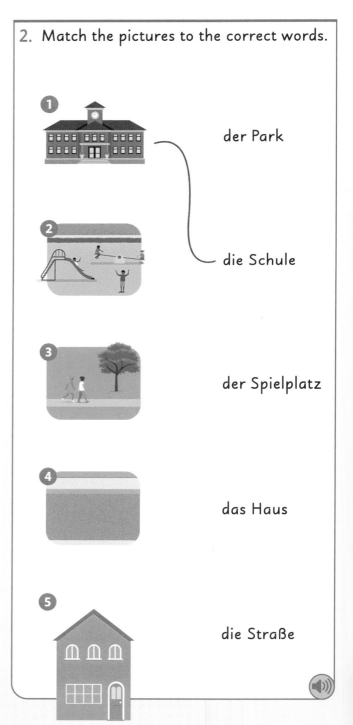

① der Park

② die Schule

③ der Spielplatz

④ das Haus

⑤ die Straße

3. Look at the numbers and write the correct words.

11

① elf ....

13

② d ....

15

③ f ....

14

④ v ....

12

⑤ z ....

4. Look at the pictures and write the correct words.

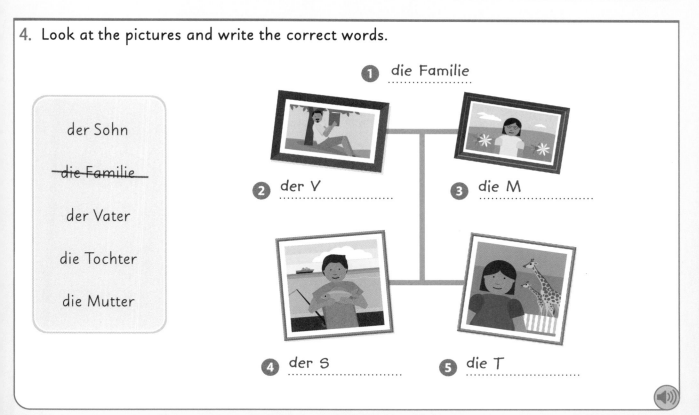

① die Familie ....

der Sohn

~~die Familie~~

der Vater

die Tochter

die Mutter

② der V ....

③ die M ....

④ der S ....

⑤ die T ....

Day 1

Listen, repeat, and copy.

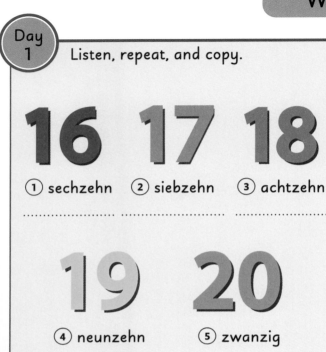

16 17 18

① sechzehn ② siebzehn ③ achtzehn

19 20

④ neunzehn ⑤ zwanzig

Listen again and write the words.

16 s ....

17 s ....

18 a ....

19 n ....

20 z ....

Day 2

Listen, repeat, and copy.

① die Kuh

② die Ziege ③ das Schaf

④ das Huhn

⑤ das Pferd

Listen again and write the words.

die K ....

die Z ....

das S ....

das H ....

das P ....

Listen again and write the words.

das S ....

das B ....

das W ....

das E ....

die K ....

Listen, repeat, and copy.

① das Schlafzimmer
....

② das Badezimmer
....

③ das Wohnzimmer
....

④ das Esszimmer
....

⑤ die Küche
....

Listen again and write the words.

s ....

w ....

b ....

r ....

o ....

Listen, repeat, and copy.

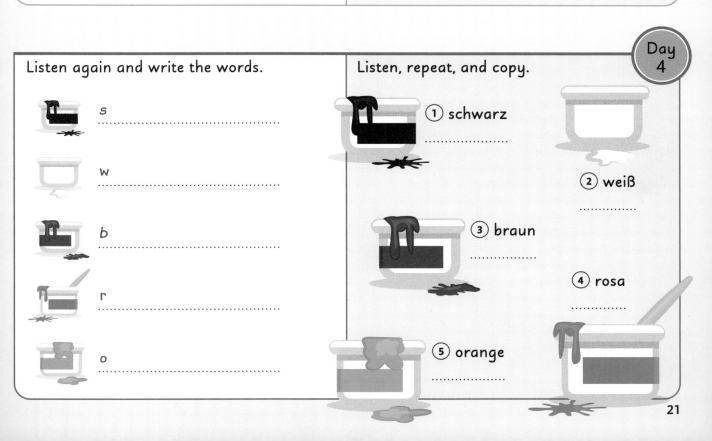

① schwarz
....

② weiß
....

③ braun
....

④ rosa
....

⑤ orange
....

Day 5

What can you remember from this week?

1. Look at the pictures and fill in the missing letters.

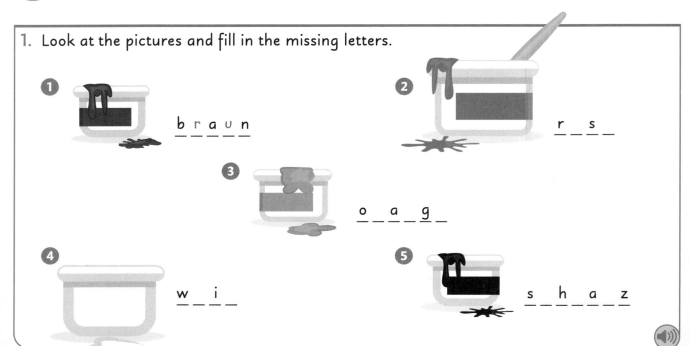

① b r a u n
_ _ _ _ _

② r _ s _
_ _ _ _

③ o _ a _ g _
_ _ _ _ _ _

④ w _ i _
_ _ _ _

⑤ s _ h _ a _ z
_ _ _ _ _ _

2. Read the words and mark the correct pictures.

① das Schlafzimmer

A ☐ B ☑

② die Küche

A ☐ B ☐

③ das Badezimmer

A ☐ B ☐

④ das Wohnzimmer

A ☐ B ☐

⑤ das Esszimmer

A ☐ B ☐

3. Look at the pictures and mark the correct words.

① die Kuh ☐
das Huhn ☑
das Schaf ☐

② das Huhn ☐
die Ziege ☐
das Pferd ☐

③ das Schaf ☐
die Kuh ☐
das Pferd ☐

④ die Ziege ☐
das Huhn ☐
die Kuh ☐

⑤ das Pferd ☐
das Schaf ☐
die Ziege ☐

4. Look at the numbers and write the letters in the correct order.

① **17**
s z i e h n b e
s i e b z e h n

② **20**
z z n i a w g
z _ _ _ _ _ _ _

③ **18**
a h n c h t z e
a _ _ _ _ _ _ _

④ **16**
s h n e h z e c
s _ _ _ _ _ _ _

⑤ **19**
n n z e h u e n
n _ _ _ _ _ _ _

Week 5

Day 1

Listen, repeat, and copy.

① das Zebra

....

② die Giraffe

....

③ der Löwe

....

④ das Nilpferd

....

⑤ der Elefant

....

Listen again and write the words.

das Z ....

die G ....

der L ....

das N ....

der E ....

Day 2

Listen, repeat, and copy.

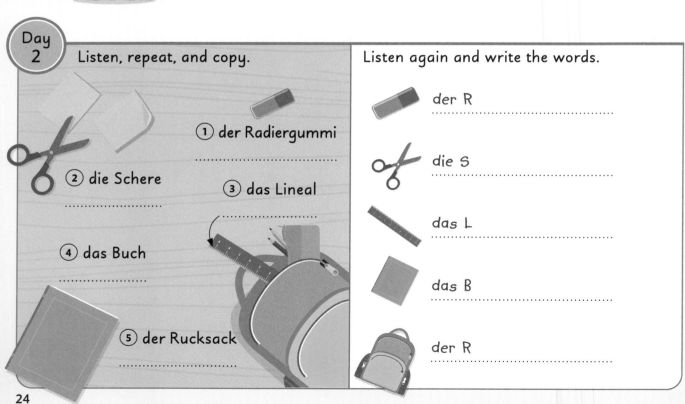

① der Radiergummi

....

② die Schere

....

③ das Lineal

....

④ das Buch

....

⑤ der Rucksack

....

Listen again and write the words.

der R ....

die S ....

das L ....

das B ....

der R ....

24

Listen again and write the words.

 a ....

 z ....

 l ....

 u ....

 z ....

Listen, repeat, and copy.

 ① antworten
....

 ② zuhören
....

 ③ lernen
....

 ④ unterrichten
....

⑤ zeigen
....

Listen again and write the words.

 die M ....

 die B ....

 die K ....

 die W ....

 die K ....

Listen, repeat, and copy.

① die Mango
....

② die Birne
....

③ die Kiwi
....

 **④** die Wassermelone
....

⑤ die Kokosnuss
....

Day 5

What can you remember from this week?

1. Match the pictures to the correct words.

①   der Löwe

②   das Zebra

③   der Elefant

④   das Nilpferd

⑤   die Giraffe

2. Look at the pictures and write the correct words.

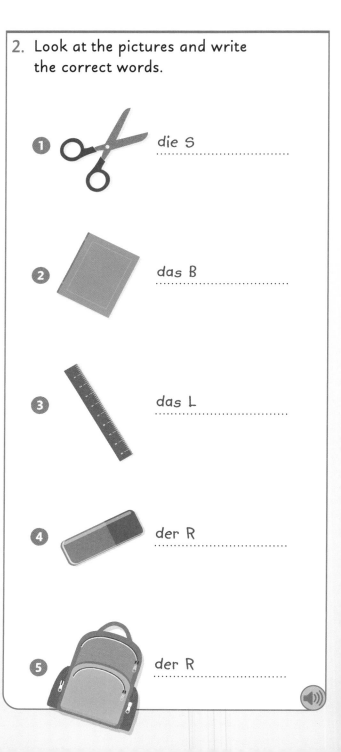

①   die S ....

②   das B ....

③   das L ....

④   der R ....

⑤   der R ....

3. Look at the pictures and write the correct words.

| antworten | zuhören | zeigen | unterrichten | lernen |

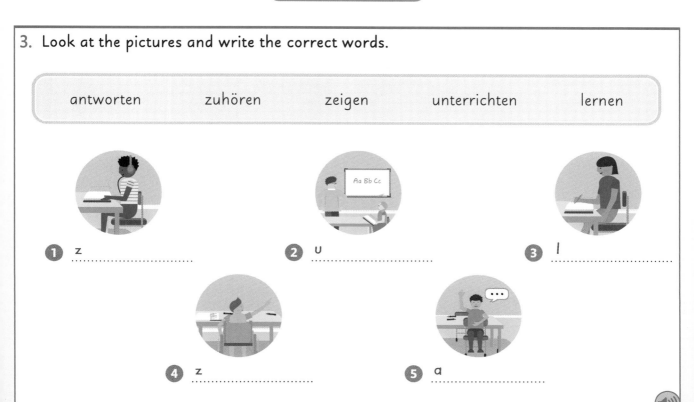

1. z _____

2. u _____

3. l _____

4. z _____

5. a _____

4. Look at the pictures and circle the correct words.

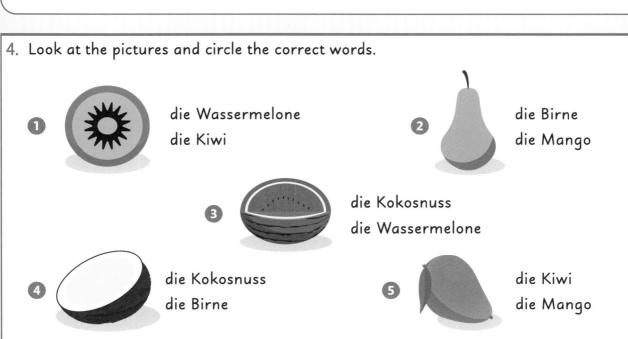

1. die Wassermelone
   die Kiwi

2. die Birne
   die Mango

3. die Kokosnuss
   die Wassermelone

4. die Kokosnuss
   die Birne

5. die Kiwi
   die Mango

Day 1

Listen, repeat, and copy.

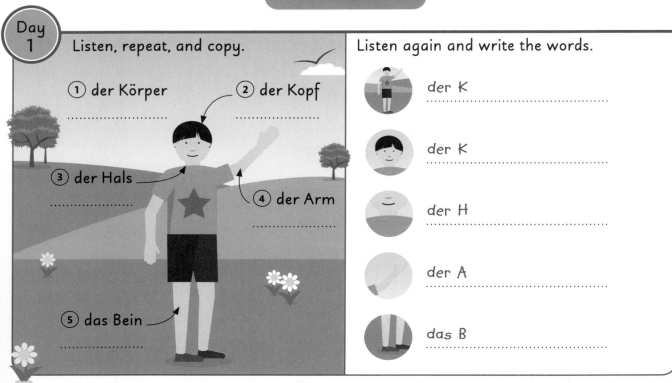

① der Körper

② der Kopf

③ der Hals

④ der Arm

⑤ das Bein

Listen again and write the words.

der K

der K

der H

der A

das B

Day 2

Listen, repeat, and copy.

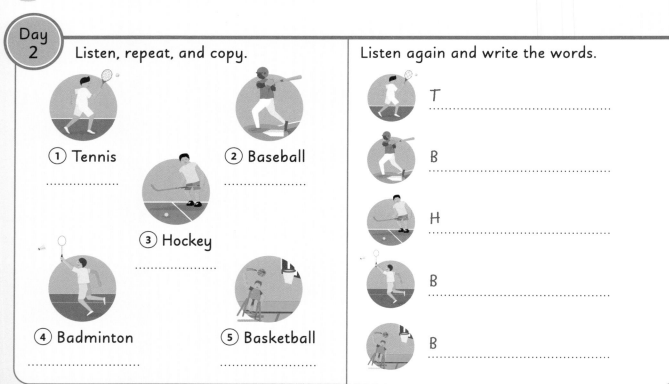

① Tennis

② Baseball

③ Hockey

④ Badminton

⑤ Basketball

Listen again and write the words.

T

B

H

B

B

Week 6

Listen again and write the words.

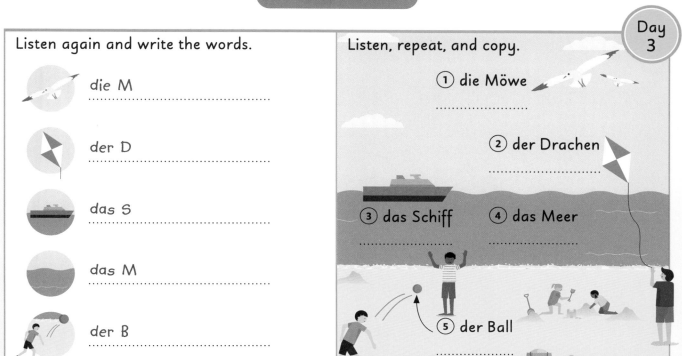

die M ....

der D ....

das S ....

das M ....

der B ....

Listen, repeat, and copy.

① die Möwe

....

② der Drachen

....

③ das Schiff   ④ das Meer

....

⑤ der Ball

....

Listen again and write the words.

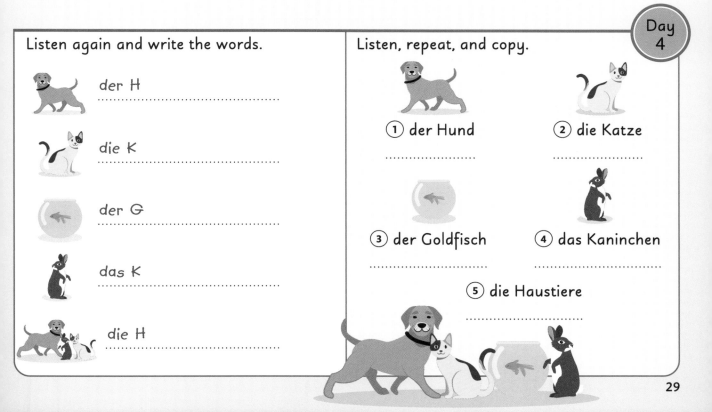

der H ....

die K ....

der G ....

das K ....

die H ....

Listen, repeat, and copy.

① der Hund   ② die Katze

....

③ der Goldfisch   ④ das Kaninchen

....

⑤ die Haustiere

....

Week 6

Day 5

What can you remember from this week?

1. Read the words and mark the correct pictures.

 **1** die Katze

A ☐   B ☐

 **2** das Kaninchen

A ☐   B ☐

3 der Hund

A ☐   B ☐

4 die Haustiere

A ☐   B ☐

5 der Goldfisch

A ☐   B ☐

2. Look at the pictures and fill in the missing letters.

 d _ r _ _ o _ f

 _ a _ B _ i _

 d _ r _ ö p _ r

 _ e _ A _ m

 d _ r _ a _ s

30

3. Look at the pictures and mark the correct words.

1. Baseball ☐
   Hockey ☐

2. Tennis ☐
   Badminton ☐

3. Basketball ☐
   Baseball ☐

4. Tennis ☐
   Basketball ☐

5. Badminton ☐
   Hockey ☐

4. Look at the pictures and write the correct words.

1. das M ....

2. die M ....

3. der D ....

4. das S ....

5. der B ....

Day 1

Listen, repeat, and copy.

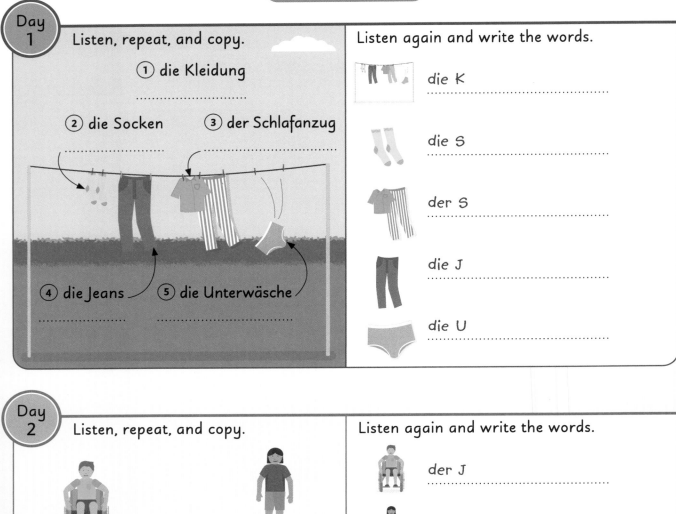

① die Kleidung

....

② die Socken   ③ der Schlafanzug

....

④ die Jeans   ⑤ die Unterwäsche

....

Listen again and write the words.

die K ....

die S ....

der S ....

die J ....

die U ....

Day 2

Listen, repeat, and copy.

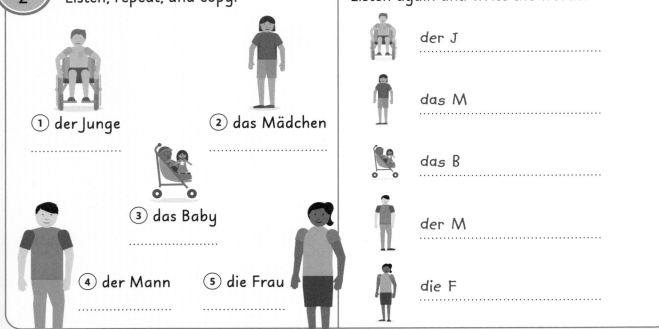

① der Junge   ② das Mädchen

....

③ das Baby

....

④ der Mann   ⑤ die Frau

....

Listen again and write the words.

der J ....

das M ....

das B ....

der M ....

die F ....

Week 7

Listen again and write the words.

der H ....

die P ....

das H ....

die P ....

die N ....

Listen, repeat, and copy.

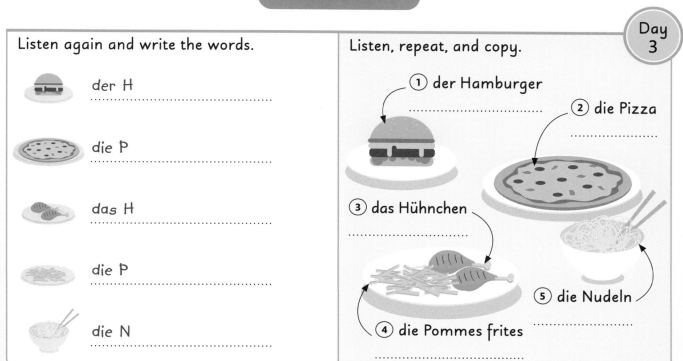

① der Hamburger ....

② die Pizza ....

③ das Hühnchen ....

④ die Pommes frites ....

⑤ die Nudeln ....

Listen again and write the words.

der F ....

der S ....

das B ....

der T ....

das S ....

Listen, repeat, and copy.

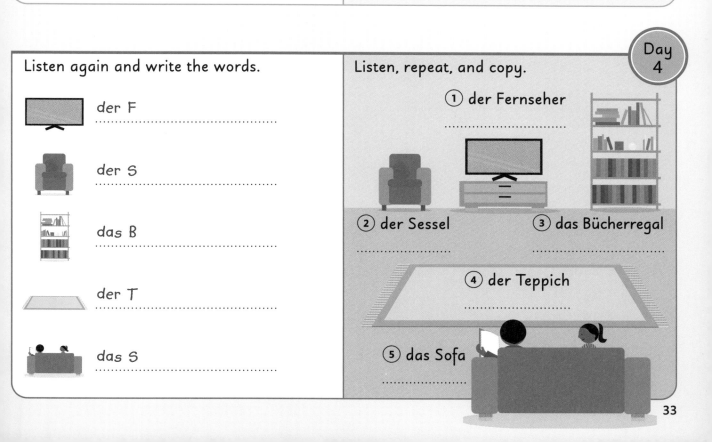

① der Fernseher ....

② der Sessel ....

③ das Bücherregal ....

④ der Teppich ....

⑤ das Sofa ....

Day 5

What can you remember from this week?

1. Look at the pictures and fill in the missing letters.

① d _ s _ ä _ c _ e _

② _ e _ _ a _ n

③ d _ _ r _ _ u _ g _

④ _ a _ B _ b _

⑤ d _ _ e _ r _ u

2. Read the words and mark the correct pictures.

① die Jeans   A ☐   B ☐

② die Unterwäsche   A ☐   B ☐

③ der Schlafanzug   A ☐   B ☐

④ die Socken   A ☐   B ☐

⑤ die Kleidung   A ☐   B ☐

3. Look at the pictures and write the correct words.

der Teppich   das Sofa   der Fernseher   das Bücherregal   der Sessel

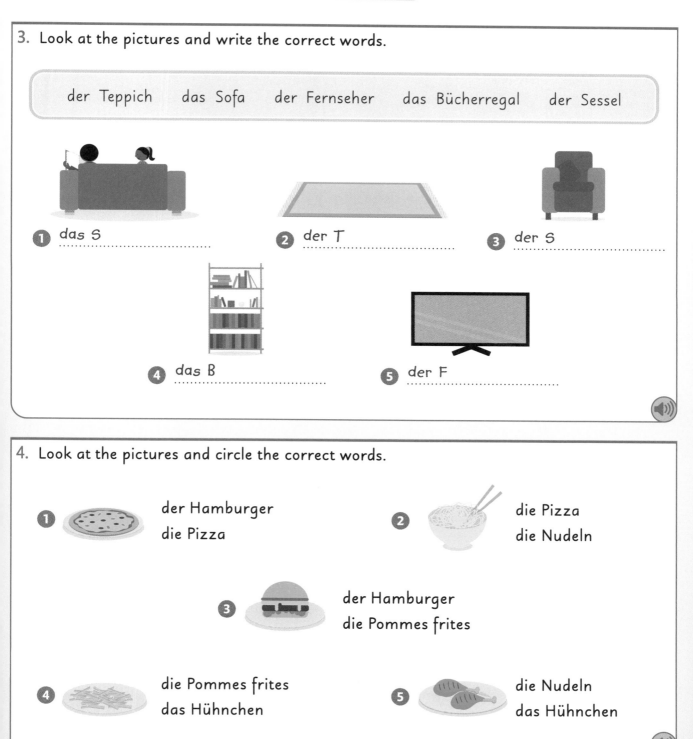

1 das S ....

2 der T ....

3 der S ....

4 das B ....

5 der F ....

4. Look at the pictures and circle the correct words.

1 der Hamburger
die Pizza

2 die Pizza
die Nudeln

3 der Hamburger
die Pommes frites

4 die Pommes frites
das Hühnchen

5 die Nudeln
das Hühnchen

Day 1

Listen, repeat, and copy.

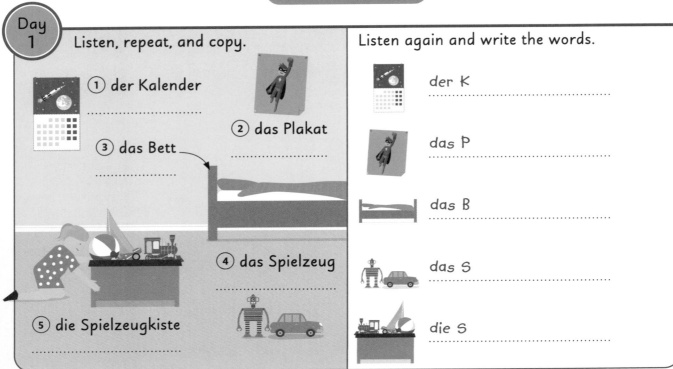

① der Kalender

② das Plakat

③ das Bett

④ das Spielzeug

⑤ die Spielzeugkiste

Listen again and write the words.

der K

das P

das B

das S

die S

Day 2

Listen, repeat, and copy.

① der Tag

② die Nacht

③ der Morgen

④ der Nachmittag

⑤ der Abend

Listen again and write the words.

der T

die N

der M

der N

der A

Listen again and write the words.

a ....

z ....

a ....

h ....

a ....

Listen, repeat, and copy.

① aufklappen
....

② zuklappen
....

③ aufnehmen
....

④ hinsetzen
....

⑤ aufstehen
....

Listen again and write the words.

der D ....

der A ....

der T ....

der B ....

der F ....

Listen, repeat, and copy.

① der Dschungel
....

② der Affe
....

③ der Tiger
....

④ der Bär
....

⑤ der Frosch
....

Day 5

What can you remember from this week?

1. Look at the pictures and write the correct words.

1 der T _____

2 der F _____

3 der A _____

4 der D _____

5 der B _____

2. Read the words and mark the correct pictures.

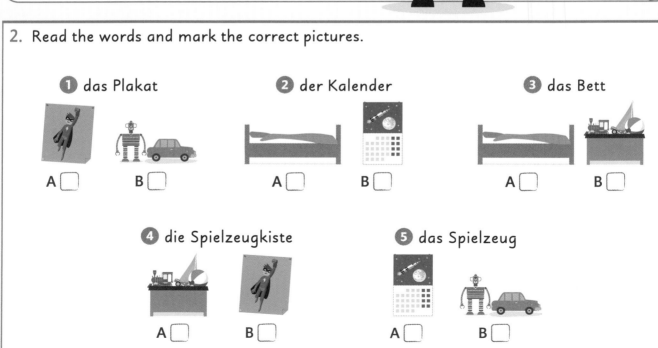

1 das Plakat
A ☐ B ☐

2 der Kalender
A ☐ B ☐

3 das Bett
A ☐ B ☐

4 die Spielzeugkiste
A ☐ B ☐

5 das Spielzeug
A ☐ B ☐

3. Look at the pictures and fill in the missing letters.

 h _ n _ e _ z _ n

 a _ f _ l _ p _ e _

 z _ k _ a _ p _ n

 a _ f _ e _ m _ n

 a _ f _ t _ h _ n

4. Look at the pictures and mark the correct words.

 der Nachmittag ☐
der Abend ☐

 die Nacht ☐
der Nachmittag ☐

 die Nacht ☐
der Morgen ☐

 der Tag ☐
der Abend ☐

 der Morgen ☐
der Tag ☐

Week 9

Day 1

Listen, repeat, and copy.

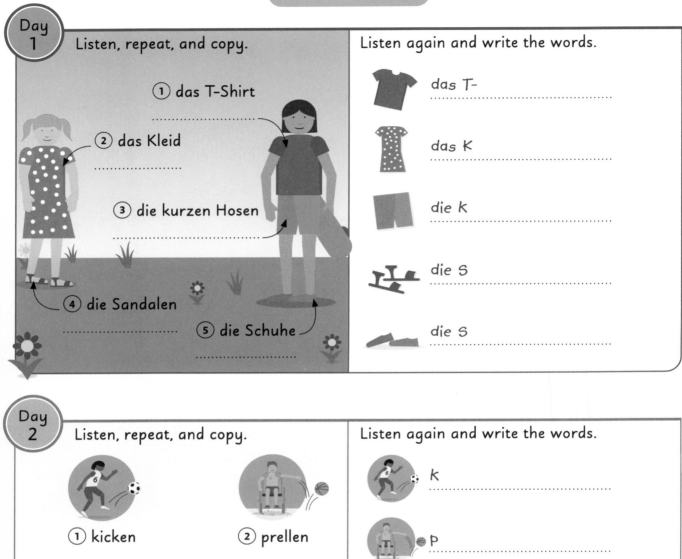

① das T-Shirt

② das Kleid

③ die kurzen Hosen

④ die Sandalen

⑤ die Schuhe

Listen again and write the words.

das T-

das K

die k

die S

die S

Day 2

Listen, repeat, and copy.

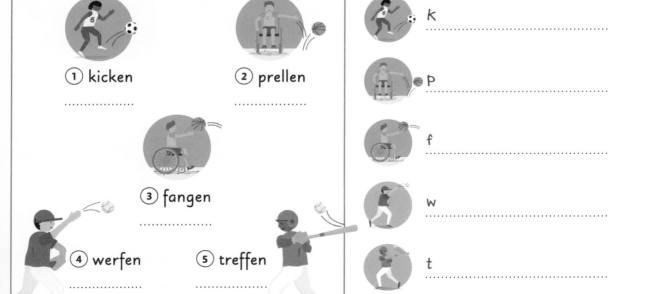

① kicken

② prellen

③ fangen

④ werfen

⑤ treffen

Listen again and write the words.

k

p

f

w

t

Week 9

Listen again and write the words.

die G ....

die G ....

der G ....

der E ....

die E ....

Listen, repeat, and copy.

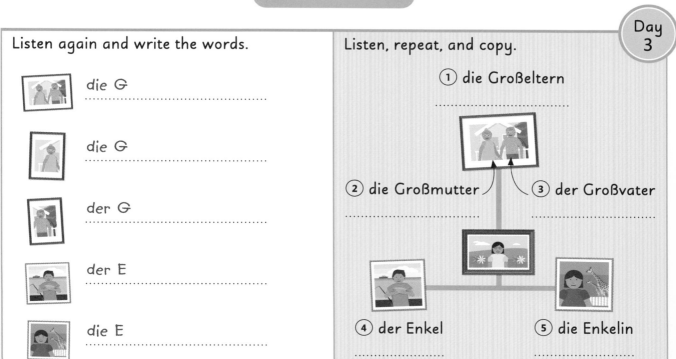

① die Großeltern ....

② die Großmutter   ③ der Großvater ....

④ der Enkel ....   ⑤ die Enkelin ....

Listen again and write the words.

h ....

j ....

a ....

n ....

a ....

Listen, repeat, and copy.

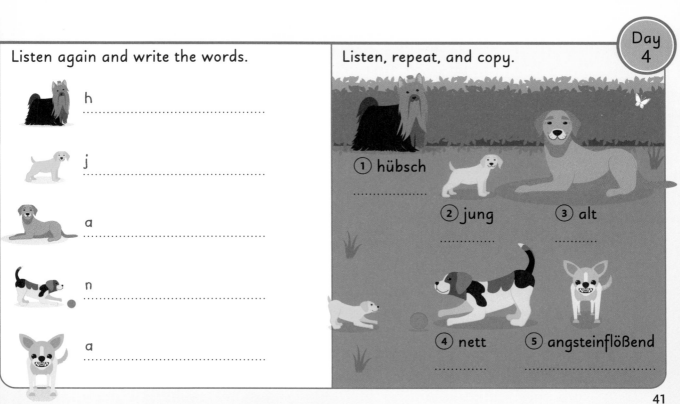

① hübsch ....

② jung ....   ③ alt ....

④ nett ....   ⑤ angsteinflößend ....

What can you remember from this week?

1. Look at the pictures and write the correct words.

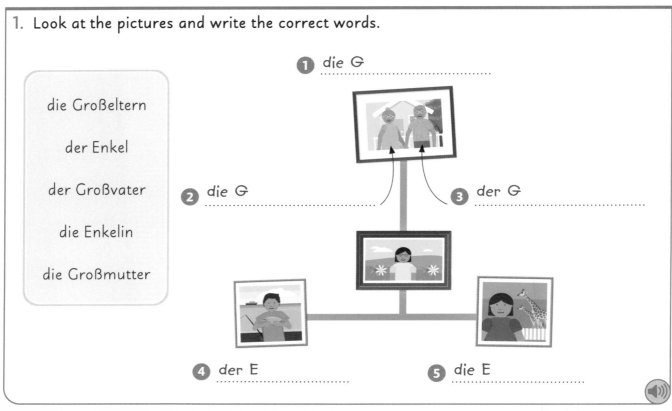

1 die G ....

die Großeltern

der Enkel

der Großvater

die Enkelin

die Großmutter

2 die G ....

3 der G ....

4 der E ....

5 die E ....

2. Match the pictures to the correct words.

1   2   3   4   5

die Sandalen   das T-Shirt   die kurzen Hosen   das Kleid   die Schuhe

3. Look at the pictures and mark the correct words.

1. hübsch ☐
   alt ☐

2. angsteinflößend ☐
   alt ☐

3. angsteinflößend ☐
   nett ☐

4. hübsch ☐
   jung ☐

5. nett ☐
   jung ☐

4. Look at the pictures and write the correct words.

kicken fangen treffen
werfen prellen

1. f _____

2. t _____

3. k _____

4. w _____

5. p _____

43

Day 1

Listen, repeat, and copy.

① der Bauernhof

② der Traktor

③ die Tiere

④ das Feld

⑤ die Scheune

Listen again and write the words.

der B

der T

die T

das F

die S

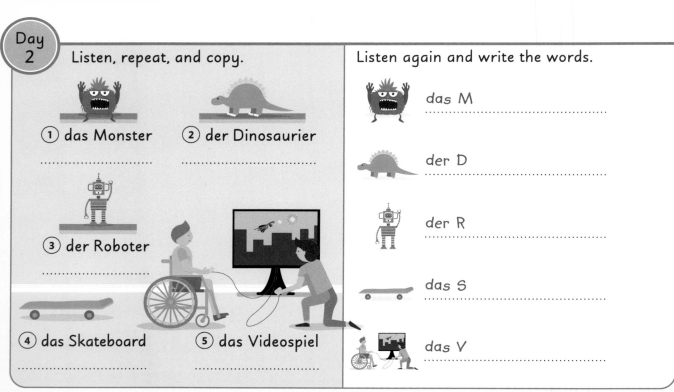

Day 2

Listen, repeat, and copy.

① das Monster

② der Dinosaurier

③ der Roboter

④ das Skateboard

⑤ das Videospiel

Listen again and write the words.

das M

der D

der R

das S

das V

Listen again and write the words.

a ....

e ....

a ....

a ....

z ....

Listen, repeat, and copy.

① ankreuzen

② einkreisen

③ abhaken

④ addieren

⑤ zuordnen

Listen again and write the words.

die M ....

die M ....

die F ....

die K ....

die P ....

Listen, repeat, and copy.

① die Männer

② die Menschen

③ die Frauen

④ die Kinder

⑤ die Person

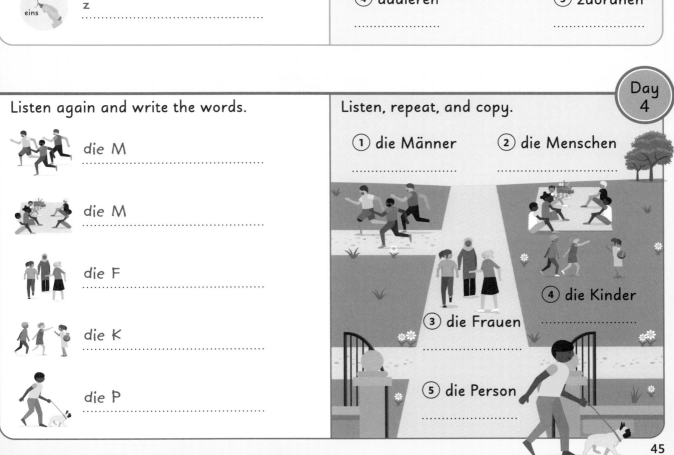

Day 5

What can you remember from this week?

1. Look at the pictures and write the letters in the correct order.

1. die P s o e r n

   die P ....

2. die F n r a u e

   die F ....

3. die K e d i n r

   die K ....

4. die M c h e n s e n

   die M ....

5. die M n e ä n r

   die M ....

2. Read the words and mark the correct pictures.

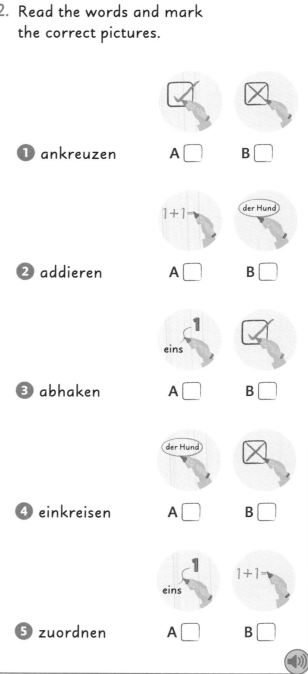

1. ankreuzen   A ☐   B ☐

2. addieren   A ☐   B ☐

3. abhaken   A ☐   B ☐

4. einkreisen   A ☐   B ☐

5. zuordnen   A ☐   B ☐

3. Look at the pictures and write the correct words.

 der T ....

 das F ....

 der B ....

 die T ....

 die S ....

4. Look at the pictures and circle the correct words.

 der Dinosaurier
der Roboter

 das Skateboard
der Dinosaurier

 das Monster
das Videospiel

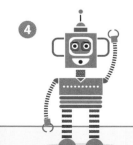 der Roboter
das Videospiel

 das Monster
das Skateboard

Day 1

Listen, repeat, and copy.

① singen

② tanzen

③ Klavier spielen

④ Gitarre spielen

⑤ ein Foto machen

Listen again and write the words.

s ....

t ....

K ....

G ....

e ....

Day 2

Listen, repeat, and copy.

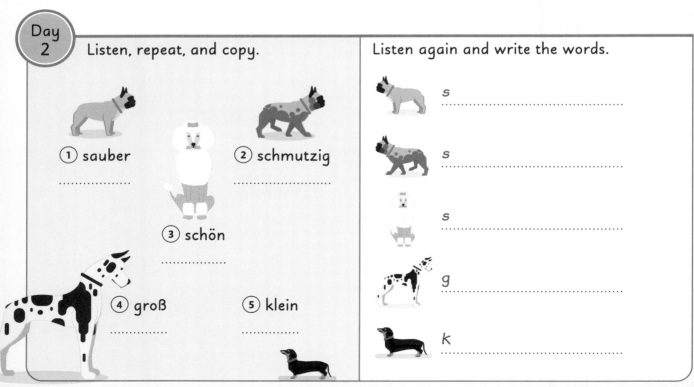

① sauber

② schmutzig

③ schön

④ groß

⑤ klein

Listen again and write the words.

s ....

s ....

s ....

g ....

k ....

Listen again and write the words.

das A ....

das O ....

das G ....

die L ....

die N ....

Listen, repeat, and copy.

① das Auge

....

② das Ohr

....

③ das Gesicht

....

④ die Lippen

....

⑤ die Nase

....

Listen again and write the words.

das H ....

der R ....

die H ....

die K ....

die J ....

Listen, repeat, and copy.

① das Hemd

....

② der Rock

....

③ die Hose

....

④ die Kappe

....

⑤ die Jacke

....

49

Day 5

What can you remember from this week?

1. Look at the pictures and write the correct words.

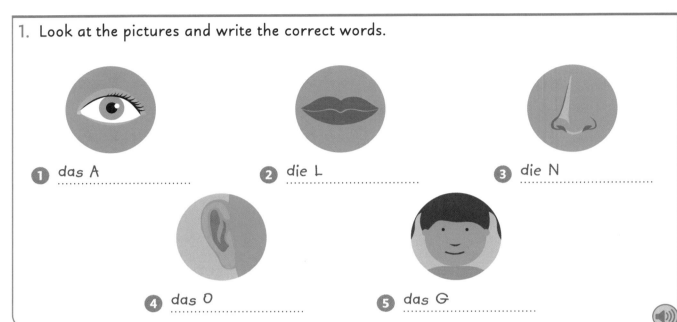

1 das A ....

2 die L ....

3 die N ....

4 das O ....

5 das G ....

2. Read the words and mark the correct pictures.

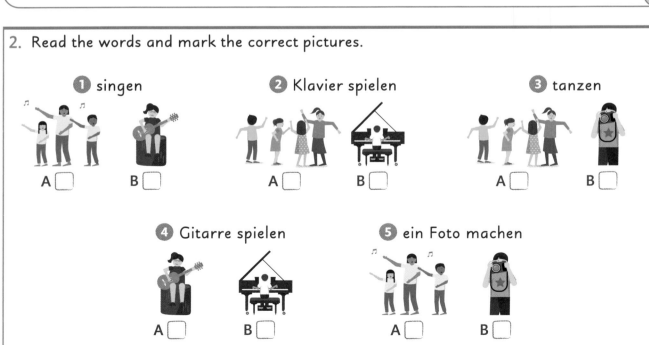

1 singen

A ☐   B ☐

2 Klavier spielen

A ☐   B ☐

3 tanzen

A ☐   B ☐

4 Gitarre spielen

A ☐   B ☐

5 ein Foto machen

A ☐   B ☐

3. Look at the pictures and write
   the letters in the correct order.

1   sönch

    s _ _ _ _ _

2   sbeaur

    s _ _ _ _ _ _

3   knlie

    k _ _ _ _ _

4   smuchtgzi

    s _ _ _ _ _ _ _ _

5   gßro

    g _ _ _

4. Match the pictures to the correct words.

1   der Rock

2   das Hemd

3   die Kappe

4   die Jacke

5   die Hose

Week 12

Day 1

Listen, repeat, and copy.

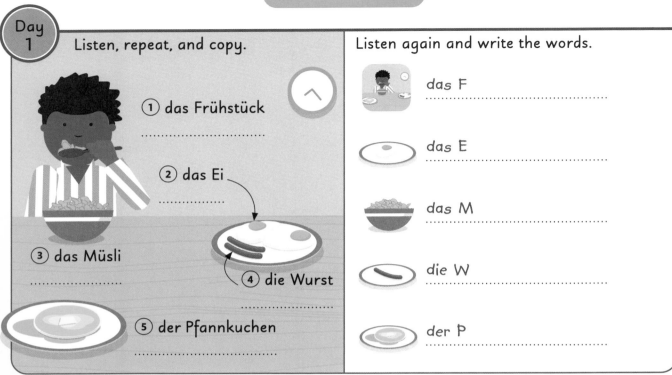

① das Frühstück
....

② das Ei
....

③ das Müsli
....

④ die Wurst
....

⑤ der Pfannkuchen
....

Listen again and write the words.

das F ....

das E ....

das M ....

die W ....

der P ....

Day 2

Listen, repeat, and copy.

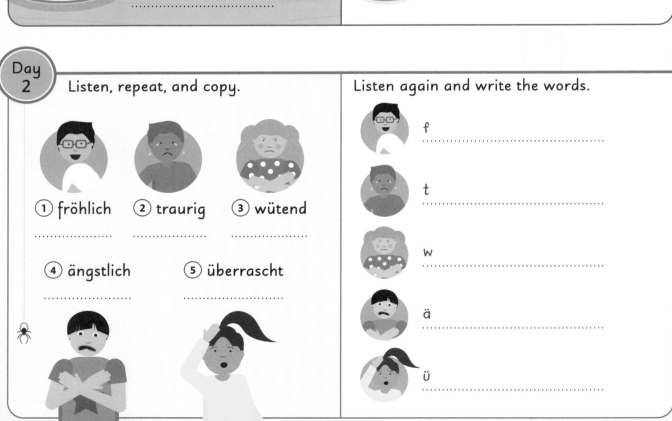

① fröhlich ② traurig ③ wütend
....

④ ängstlich ⑤ überrascht
....

Listen again and write the words.

f ....

t ....

w ....

ä ....

ü ....

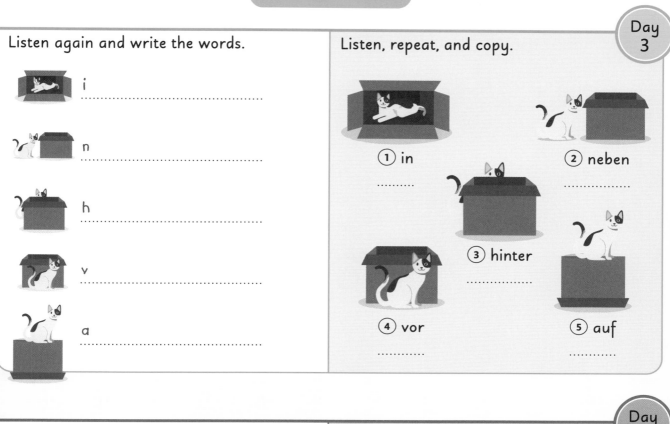

Listen again and write the words.

i ....

n ....

h ....

v ....

a ....

Listen, repeat, and copy.

1 in
....

2 neben
....

3 hinter
....

4 vor
....

5 auf
....

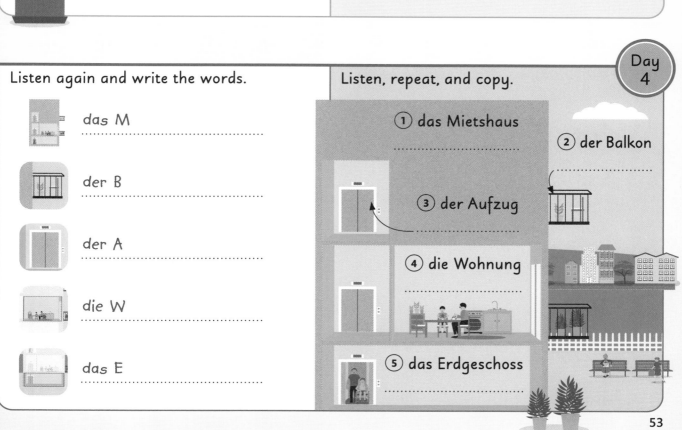

Listen again and write the words.

das M ....

der B ....

der A ....

die W ....

das E ....

Listen, repeat, and copy.

1 das Mietshaus
....

2 der Balkon
....

3 der Aufzug
....

4 die Wohnung
....

5 das Erdgeschoss
....

Day 5 What can you remember from this week?

1. Look at the pictures and write the correct words.

| in | hinter | auf |
| vor | | neben |

1   i ....

2   v ....

3   h ....

4   n ....

5   a ....

2. Look at the pictures and mark the correct words.

1   das Müsli ☐
     das Ei ☐

2   der Pfannkuchen ☐
     das Frühstück ☐

3   das Ei ☐
     die Wurst ☐

4   der Pfannkuchen ☐
     das Müsli ☐

5   das Frühstück ☐
     die Wurst ☐

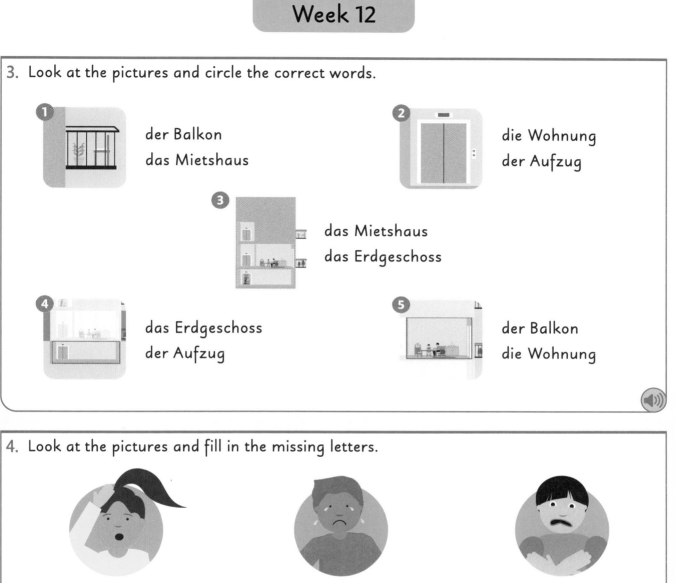

3. Look at the pictures and circle the correct words.

1. der Balkon
   das Mietshaus

2. die Wohnung
   der Aufzug

3. das Mietshaus
   das Erdgeschoss

4. das Erdgeschoss
   der Aufzug

5. der Balkon
   die Wohnung

4. Look at the pictures and fill in the missing letters.

1. ü _ e _ r _ s _ h _

2. t _ a _ r _ g

3. ä _ g _ t _ i _ h

4. f _ ö _ l _ c _

5. w _ t _ n _

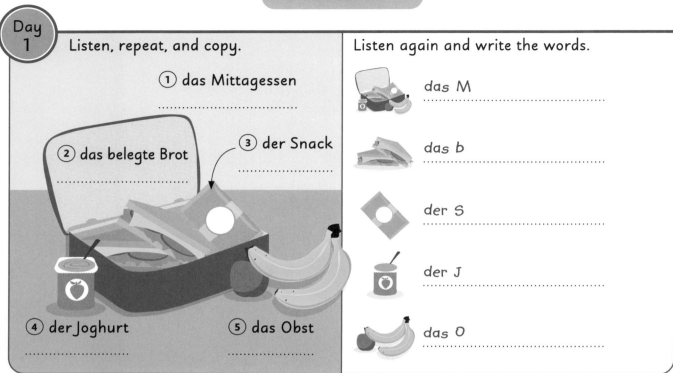

Day 1

Listen, repeat, and copy.

① das Mittagessen
....

② das belegte Brot
....

③ der Snack
....

④ der Joghurt
....

⑤ das Obst
....

Listen again and write the words.

das M ....

das b ....

der S ....

der J ....

das O ....

Day 2

Listen, repeat, and copy.

① der Baum
....

② das Blatt
....

③ der Ast
....

④ die Blume
....

⑤ die Pflanze
....

Listen again and write the words.

der B ....

das B ....

der A ....

die B ....

die P ....

Week 13

Listen again and write the words.

f ....

d ....

z ....

l ....

R ....

Listen, repeat, and copy.

① fahren

....

② den Bus nehmen

....

③ zu Fuß gehen

....

④ laufen

....

⑤ Rad fahren

....

Listen again and write the words.

der R ....

der S ....

der W ....

der N ....

der R ....

Listen, repeat, and copy.

① der Regen

....

② der Sturm

....

③ der Wind

....

④ der Nebel

....

⑤ der Regenbogen

....

What can you remember from this week?

1. Read the words and mark the correct pictures.

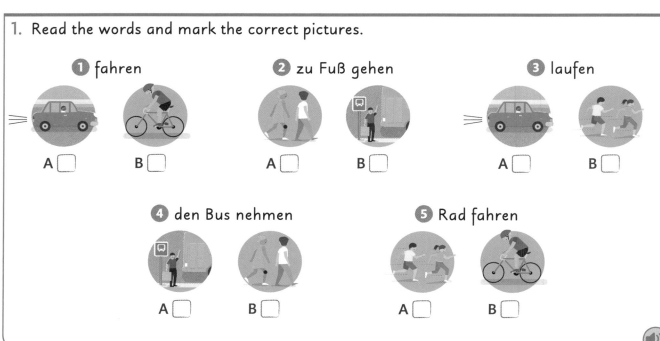

❶ fahren

A ☐   B ☐

❷ zu Fuß gehen

A ☐   B ☐

❸ laufen

A ☐   B ☐

❹ den Bus nehmen

A ☐   B ☐

❺ Rad fahren

A ☐   B ☐

2. Look at the pictures and write the correct words.

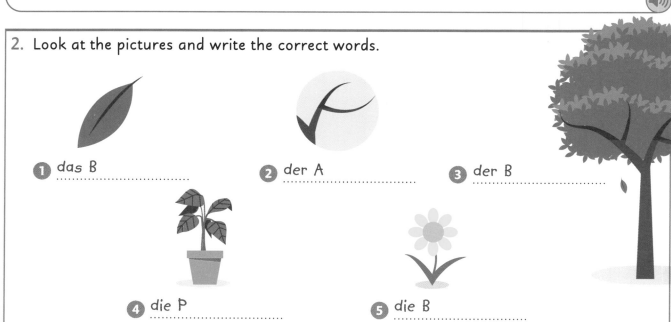

❶ das B ....

❷ der A ....

❸ der B ....

❹ die P ....

❺ die B ....

3. Look at the pictures and write the correct words.

der Regen   der Sturm   der Wind
der Regenbogen   der Nebel

 der S ....

 der W ....

 der N ....

 der R ....

 der R ....

4. Match the pictures to the correct words.

 das Obst

 der Snack

 das Mittagessen

 der Joghurt

 das belegte Brot

Week 14

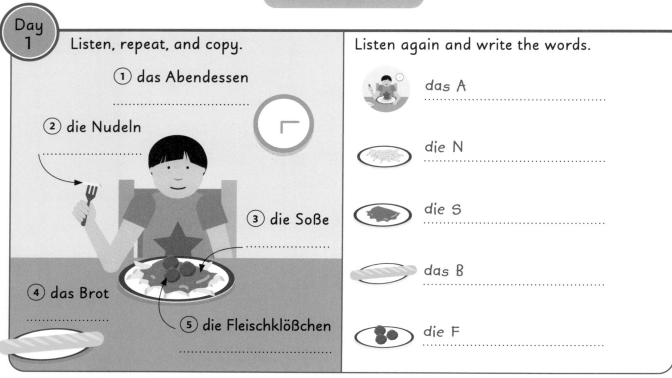

Day 1

Listen, repeat, and copy.

1. das Abendessen
2. die Nudeln
3. die Soße
4. das Brot
5. die Fleischklößchen

Listen again and write the words.

das A

die N

die S

das B

die F

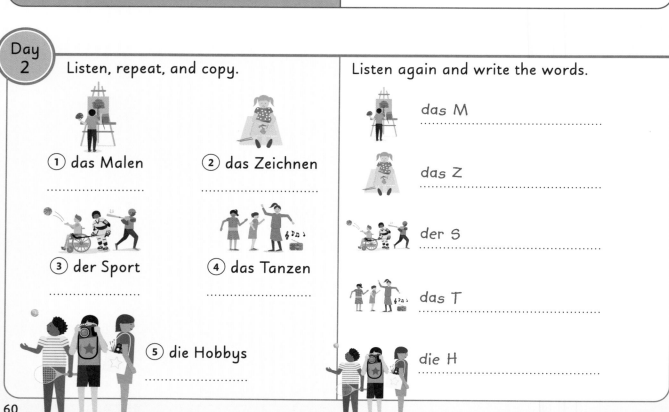

Day 2

Listen, repeat, and copy.

1. das Malen
2. das Zeichnen
3. der Sport
4. das Tanzen
5. die Hobbys

Listen again and write the words.

das M

das Z

der S

das T

die H

Week 14

Listen again and write the words.

der O ....

die T ....

die C ....

der B ....

die S ....

Listen, repeat, and copy.

① der Onkel ....

② die Tante ....

③ die Cousine ....

④ der Bruder ....

⑤ die Schwester ....

Listen again and write the words.

das D ....

die H ....

das Z ....

der G ....

der Z ....

Listen, repeat, and copy.

① das Dach ....

② die Hütte ....

③ das Zuhause ....

④ der Garten ....

⑤ der Zaun ....

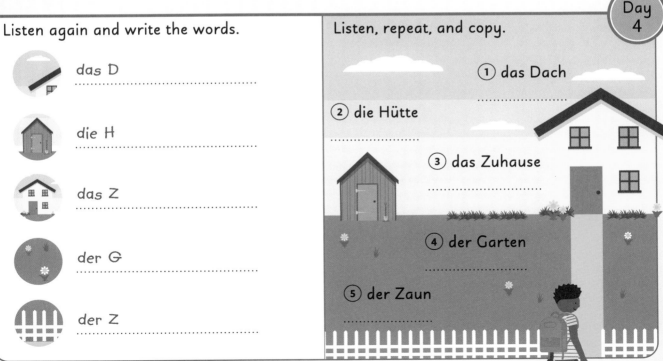

Day 5

What can you remember from this week?

---

1. Look at the pictures and circle the correct words.

das Dach / der Garten

die Hütte / der Zaun

der Garten / das Zuhause

das Dach / die Hütte

das Zuhause / der Zaun

---

2. Look at the pictures and write the letters in the correct order.

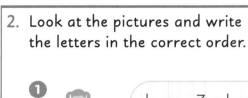
das Zchneien

das Z _ _ _ _ _ _ _

das Tzanne

das T _ _ _ _ _ _

das Mlena

das M _ _ _ _ _

der Srtpo

der S _ _ _ _ _

die Hbyobs

die H _ _ _ _ _ _

3. Look at the pictures and write the correct words.

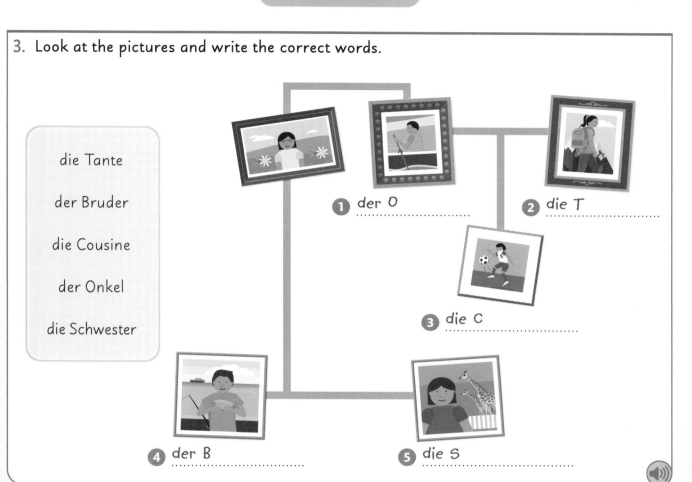

die Tante

der Bruder

die Cousine

der Onkel

die Schwester

1 der O ....

2 die T ....

3 die C ....

4 der B ....

5 die S ....

4. Match the pictures to the correct words.

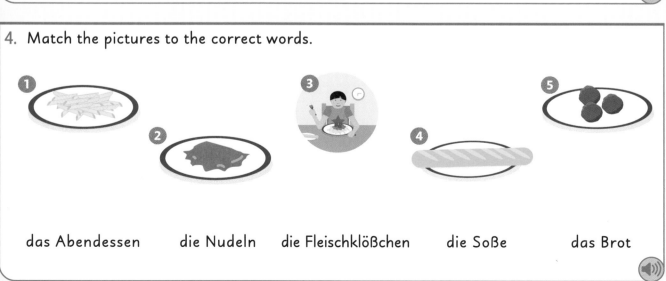

das Abendessen   die Nudeln   die Fleischklößchen   die Soße   das Brot

Week 15

Day 1

Listen, repeat, and copy.

① spielen

② klettern

③ laufen

④ springen

⑤ seilspringen

Listen again and write the words.

s ....

k ....

l ....

s ....

s ....

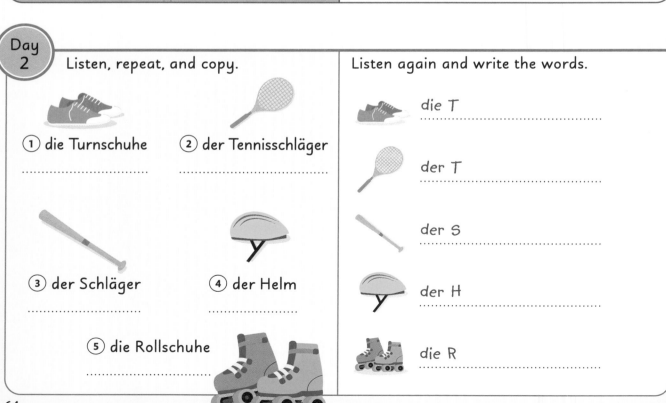

Day 2

Listen, repeat, and copy.

① die Turnschuhe

② der Tennisschläger

③ der Schläger

④ der Helm

⑤ die Rollschuhe

Listen again and write the words.

die T ....

der T ....

der S ....

der H ....

die R ....

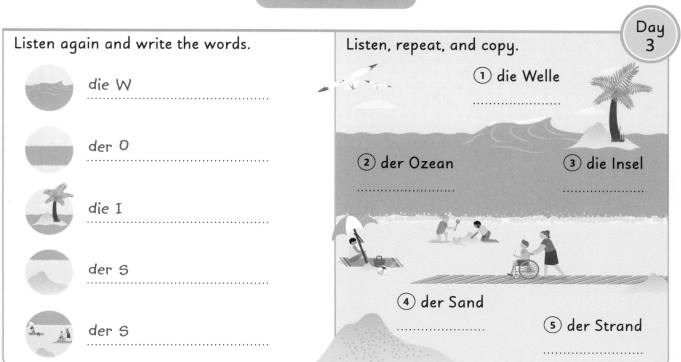

Day 3

Listen again and write the words.

die W

der O

die I

der S

der S

Listen, repeat, and copy.

① die Welle

② der Ozean

③ die Insel

④ der Sand

⑤ der Strand

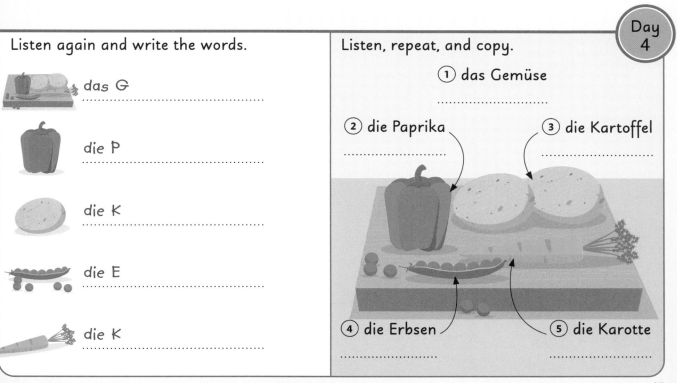

Day 4

Listen again and write the words.

das G

die P

die K

die E

die K

Listen, repeat, and copy.

① das Gemüse

② die Paprika

③ die Kartoffel

④ die Erbsen

⑤ die Karotte

Day 5

What can you remember from this week?

1. Look at the pictures and mark the correct words.

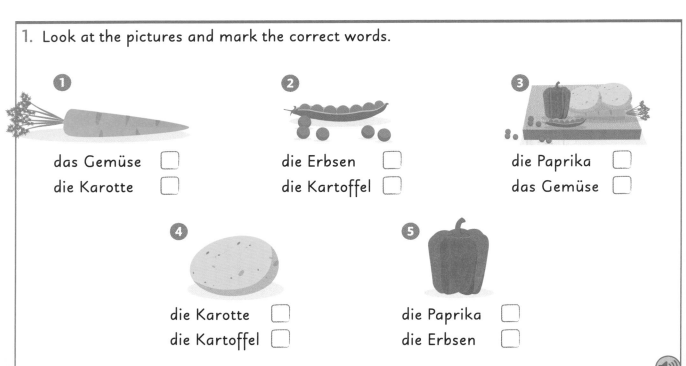

① das Gemüse ☐
die Karotte ☐

② die Erbsen ☐
die Kartoffel ☐

③ die Paprika ☐
das Gemüse ☐

④ die Karotte ☐
die Kartoffel ☐

⑤ die Paprika ☐
die Erbsen ☐

2. Look at the pictures and fill in the missing letters.

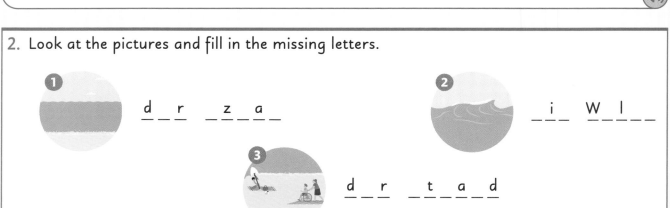

① d _ r _ _ z _ a _

② _ i _ W _ l _ _ _

③ d _ r _ _ _ t _ a _ d

④ _ e _ _ S _ n _

⑤ d _ _ e _ n _ e _

3. Match the pictures to the correct words.

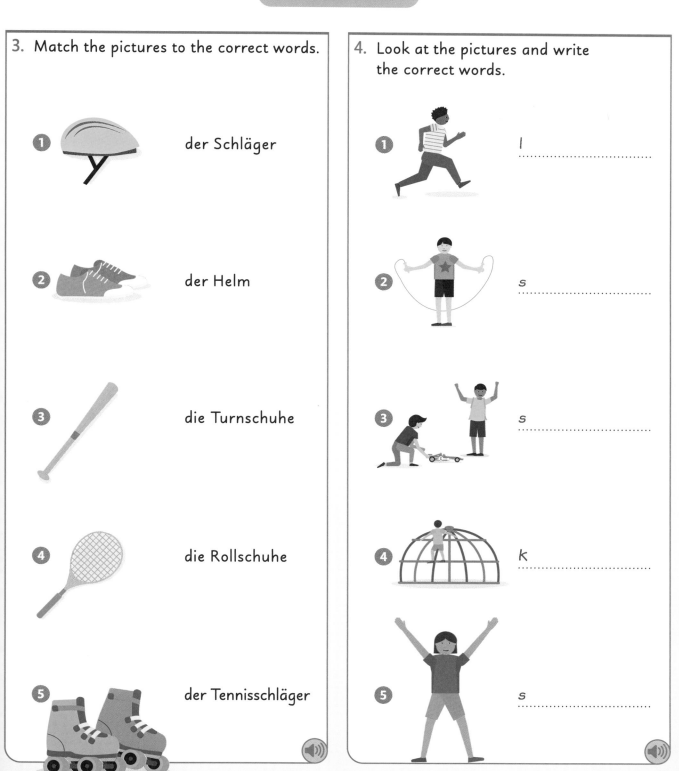

1   der Schläger

2   der Helm

3   die Turnschuhe

4   die Rollschuhe

5   der Tennisschläger

4. Look at the pictures and write the correct words.

1   l ....

2   s ....

3   s ....

4   k ....

5   s ....

Week 16

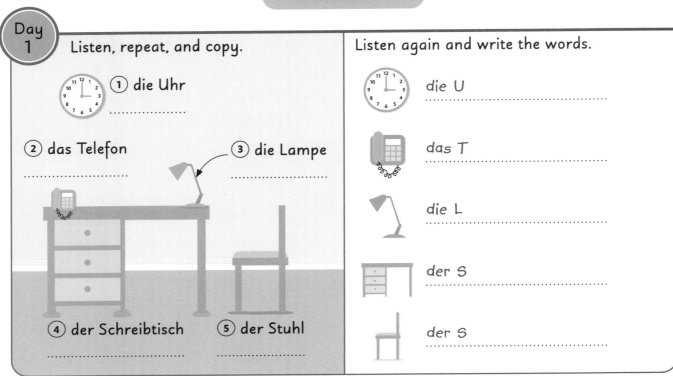

Day 1

Listen, repeat, and copy.

① die Uhr

② das Telefon

③ die Lampe

④ der Schreibtisch

⑤ der Stuhl

Listen again and write the words.

die U

das T

die L

der S

der S

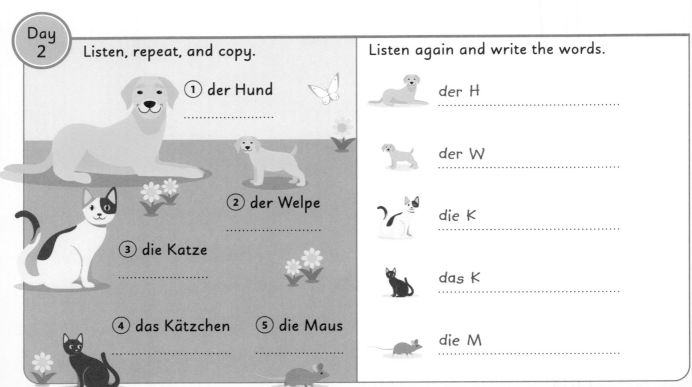

Day 2

Listen, repeat, and copy.

① der Hund

② der Welpe

③ die Katze

④ das Kätzchen

⑤ die Maus

Listen again and write the words.

der H

der W

die K

das K

die M

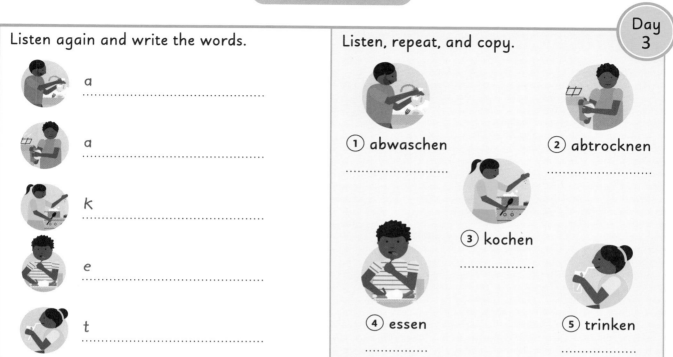

Listen again and write the words.

a ....

a ....

k ....

e ....

t ....

Listen, repeat, and copy.

1 abwaschen ....

2 abtrocknen ....

3 kochen ....

4 essen ....

5 trinken ....

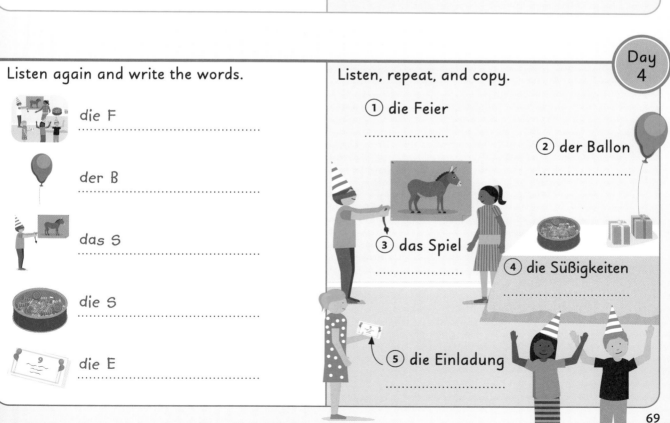

Listen again and write the words.

die F ....

der B ....

das S ....

die S ....

die E ....

Listen, repeat, and copy.

1 die Feier ....

2 der Ballon ....

3 das Spiel ....

4 die Süßigkeiten ....

5 die Einladung ....

Week 16

Day 5 What can you remember from this week?

1. Look at the pictures and mark the correct words.

① die Süßigkeiten ☐
das Spiel ☐

② der Ballon ☐
die Feier ☐

③ die Feier ☐
das Spiel ☐

④ die Einladung ☐
die Süßigkeiten ☐

⑤ die Einladung ☐
der Ballon ☐

2. Look at the pictures and write the letters in the correct order.

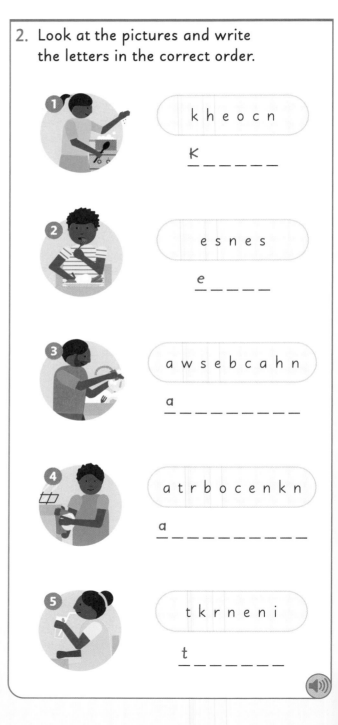

① k h e o c n
K _ _ _ _ _

② e s n e s
e _ _ _ _

③ a w s e b c a h n
a _ _ _ _ _ _ _ _

④ a t r b o c e n k n
a _ _ _ _ _ _ _ _ _

⑤ t k r n e n i
t _ _ _ _ _ _

3. Look at the pictures and write the correct words.

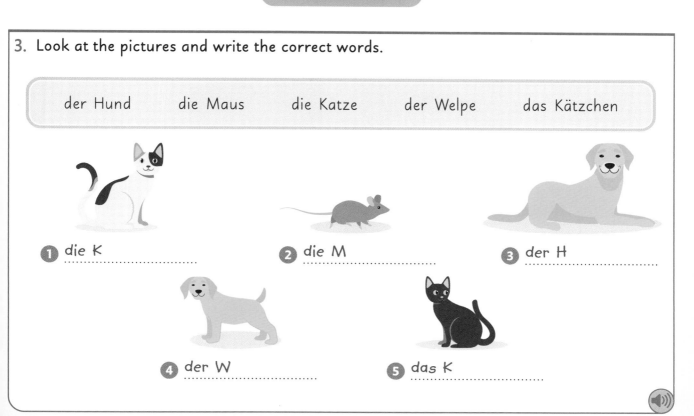

der Hund   die Maus   die Katze   der Welpe   das Kätzchen

1 die K ....

2 die M ....

3 der H ....

4 der W ....

5 das K ....

4. Look at the pictures and circle the correct words.

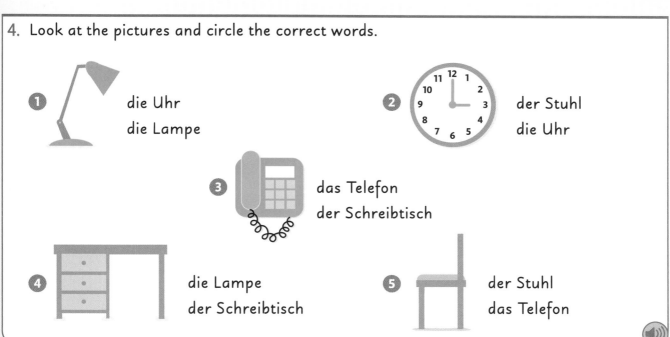

1 die Uhr
die Lampe

2 der Stuhl
die Uhr

3 das Telefon
der Schreibtisch

4 die Lampe
der Schreibtisch

5 der Stuhl
das Telefon

Day 1

Listen, repeat, and copy.

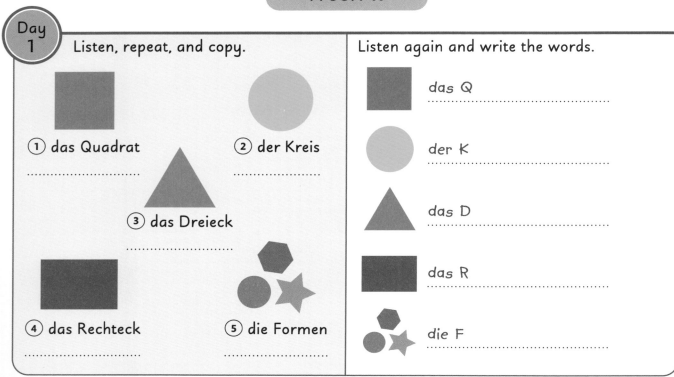

① das Quadrat

....

② der Kreis

....

③ das Dreieck

....

④ das Rechteck

....

⑤ die Formen

....

Listen again and write the words.

das Q ....

der K ....

das D ....

das R ....

die F ....

Day 2

Listen, repeat, and copy.

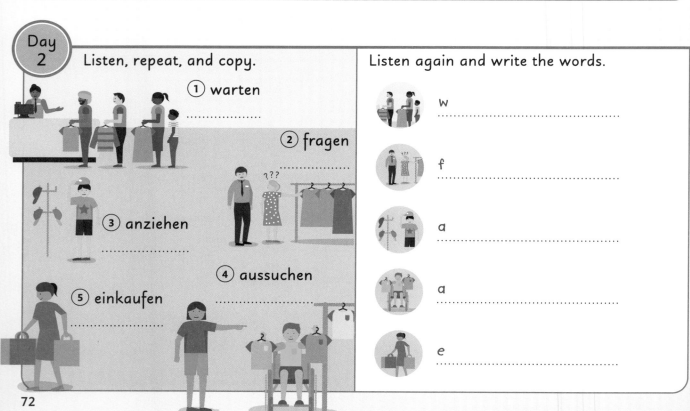

① warten

....

② fragen

....

③ anziehen

....

④ aussuchen

....

⑤ einkaufen

....

Listen again and write the words.

w ....

f ....

a ....

a ....

e ....

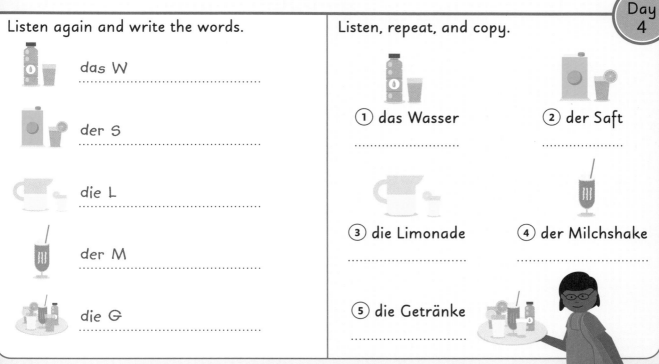

Day 3

Listen again and write the words.

die L

die R

die B

der M

die A

Listen, repeat, and copy.

① die Libelle

② die Raupe

③ die Biene

④ der Marienkäfer

⑤ die Ameise

Day 4

Listen again and write the words.

das W

der S

die L

der M

die G

Listen, repeat, and copy.

① das Wasser

② der Saft

③ die Limonade

④ der Milchshake

⑤ die Getränke

73

Day 5

What can you remember from this week?

1. Match the pictures to the correct words.

1. warten

2. fragen

3. einkaufen

4. aussuchen

5. anziehen

2. Look at the pictures and mark the correct words.

1.
- die Biene ☐
- der Marienkäfer ☐
- die Libelle ☐

2.
- die Raupe ☐
- die Ameise ☐
- die Biene ☐

3.
- die Ameise ☐
- die Libelle ☐
- der Marienkäfer ☐

4.
- die Raupe ☐
- die Biene ☐
- die Libelle ☐

5.
- der Marienkäfer ☐
- die Raupe ☐
- die Ameise ☐

3. Look at the pictures and write the correct words.

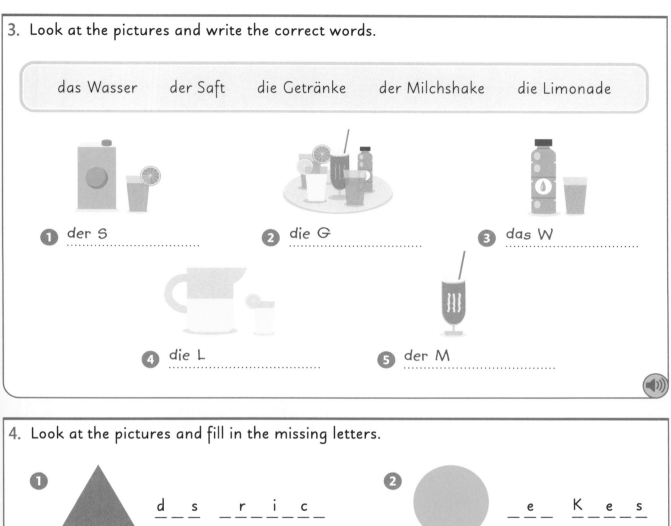

> das Wasser   der Saft   die Getränke   der Milchshake   die Limonade

1 der S ....

2 die G ....

3 das W ....

4 die L ....

5 der M ....

4. Look at the pictures and fill in the missing letters.

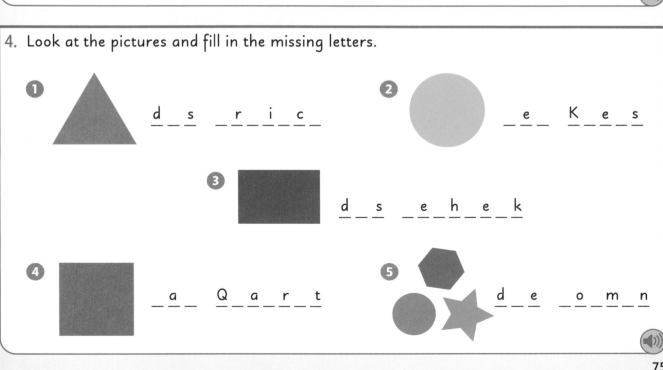

1 d _ s _ r i c _

2 _ e _ K e _ s

3 d _ s _ _ _ e h e k

4 _ a _ Q a r t

5 d _ e _ o m _ n

Day 1

Listen, repeat, and copy.

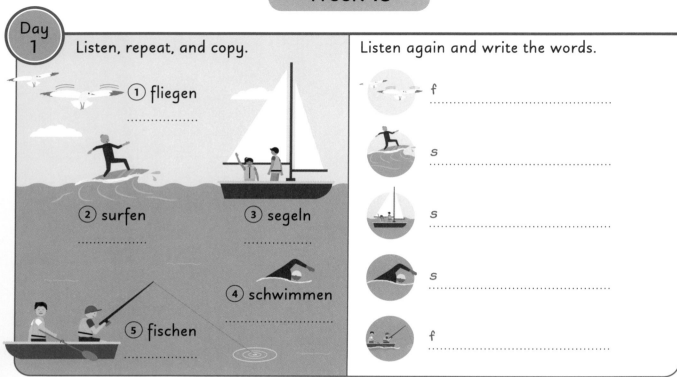

① fliegen

② surfen

③ segeln

④ schwimmen

⑤ fischen

Listen again and write the words.

f ....

s ....

s ....

s ....

f ....

Day 2

Listen, repeat, and copy.

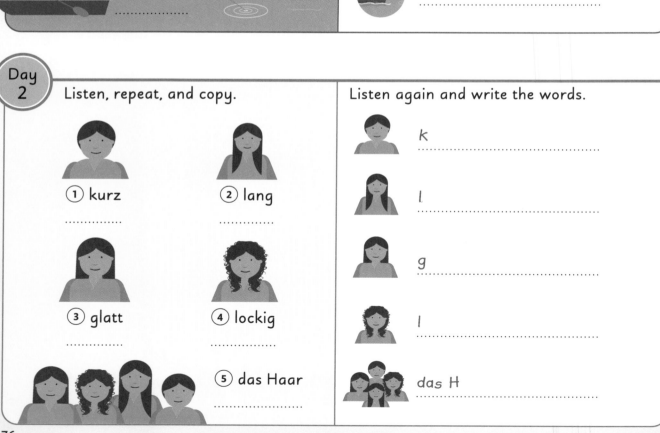

① kurz

② lang

③ glatt

④ lockig

⑤ das Haar

Listen again and write the words.

k ....

l ....

g ....

l ....

das H ....

Listen again and write the words.

die T ....

der F ....

die Ä ....

der K ....

die P ....

Listen, repeat, and copy.

① die Tierärztin ② der Feuerwehrmann

....

③ die Ärztin ④ der Krankenpfleger

....

⑤ die Polizistin

....

Listen again and write the words.

die G ....

der E ....

das K ....

die F ....

die E ....

Listen, repeat, and copy.

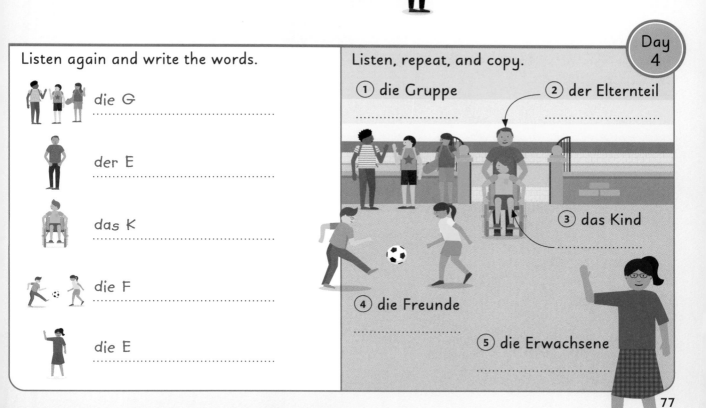

① die Gruppe ② der Elternteil

....

③ das Kind

....

④ die Freunde

....

⑤ die Erwachsene

Day 5 What can you remember from this week?

1. Read the words and mark the correct pictures.

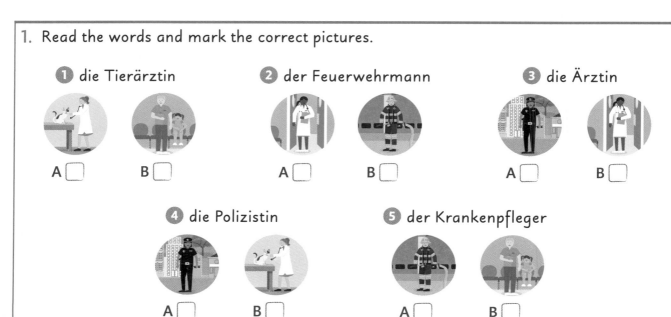

❶ die Tierärztin

A ☐   B ☐

❷ der Feuerwehrmann

A ☐   B ☐

❸ die Ärztin

A ☐   B ☐

❹ die Polizistin

A ☐   B ☐

❺ der Krankenpfleger

A ☐   B ☐

2. Look at the picture and write the correct words.

lang

lockig

das Haar

kurz

glatt

❶ das H ....

❷ k ....

❸ l ....

❹ g ....

❺ l ....

3. Look at the pictures and write the letters in the correct order.

s e n r u f

s _ _ _ _ _

f c h e i s n

f _ _ _ _ _ _

f n l g i e e

f _ _ _ _ _ _

s m w i c h m n e

s _ _ _ _ _ _ _ _

s g n e e l

s _ _ _ _ _

4. Look at the pictures and circle the correct words.

der Elternteil

das Kind

die Erwachsene

die Gruppe

die Freunde

der Elternteil

das Kind

die Gruppe

die Freunde

die Erwachsene

Day 1

Listen, repeat, and copy.

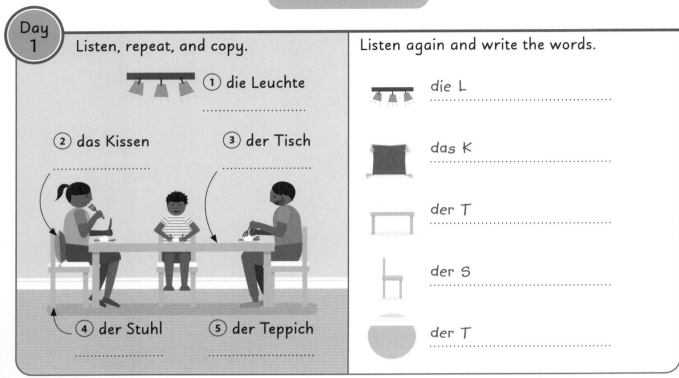

① die Leuchte

② das Kissen

③ der Tisch

④ der Stuhl

⑤ der Teppich

Listen again and write the words.

die L ....

das K ....

der T ....

der S ....

der T ....

Day 2

Listen, repeat, and copy.

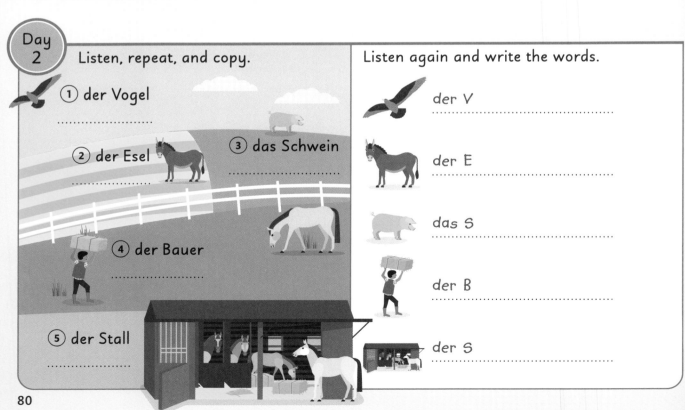

① der Vogel

② der Esel

③ das Schwein

④ der Bauer

⑤ der Stall

Listen again and write the words.

der V ....

der E ....

das S ....

der B ....

der S ....

Listen again and write the words.

k ....

w ....

s ....

b ....

g ....

Listen, repeat, and copy.

① klatschen ....

② winken ....

③ sich bewegen ....

④ berühren ....

⑤ gehen ....

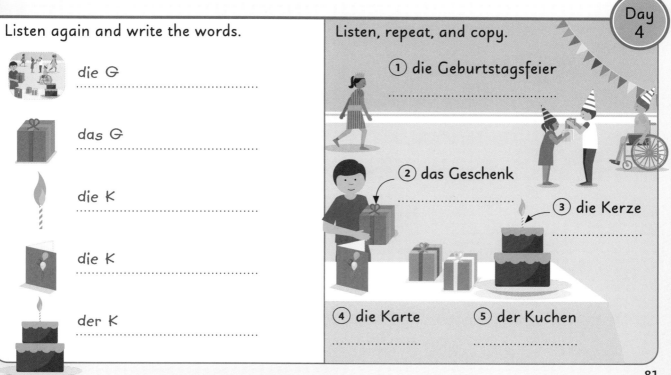

Listen again and write the words.

die G ....

das G ....

die K ....

die K ....

der K ....

Listen, repeat, and copy.

① die Geburtstagsfeier ....

② das Geschenk ....

③ die Kerze ....

④ die Karte ....

⑤ der Kuchen ....

Day 5

What can you remember from this week?

1. Match the pictures to the correct words.

1   klatschen

2   sich bewegen

3   gehen

4   winken

5   berühren

2. Look at the pictures and write the correct words.

| der Vogel | der Esel | der Stall |
| der Bauer | das Schwein |

1   der V

2   der E

3   der S

4   das S

5   der B

3. Look at the pictures and circle the correct words.

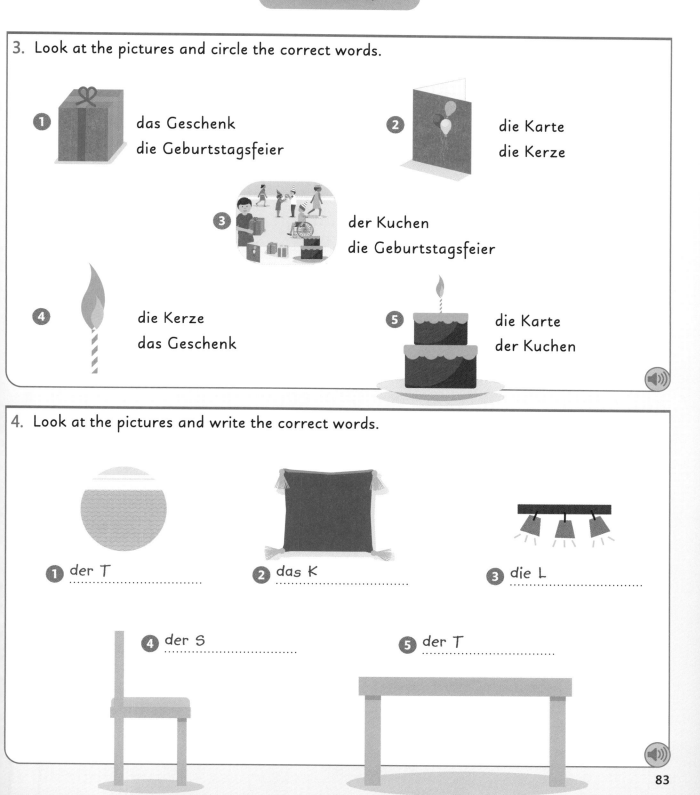

1. das Geschenk
   die Geburtstagsfeier

2. die Karte
   die Kerze

3. der Kuchen
   die Geburtstagsfeier

4. die Kerze
   das Geschenk

5. die Karte
   der Kuchen

4. Look at the pictures and write the correct words.

1. der T _____

2. das K _____

3. die L _____

4. der S _____

5. der T _____

Day 1

Listen, repeat, and copy.

① Ski fahren ② Fahrrad fahren

③ treffen ④ Schlittschuh laufen

⑤ Skateboard fahren

Listen again and write the words.

S

F

t

S

S

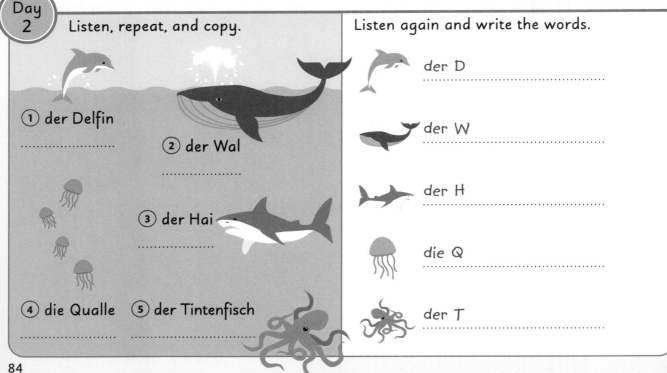

Day 2

Listen, repeat, and copy.

① der Delfin

② der Wal

③ der Hai

④ die Qualle ⑤ der Tintenfisch

Listen again and write the words.

der D

der W

der H

die Q

der T

Week 20

Listen again and write the words.

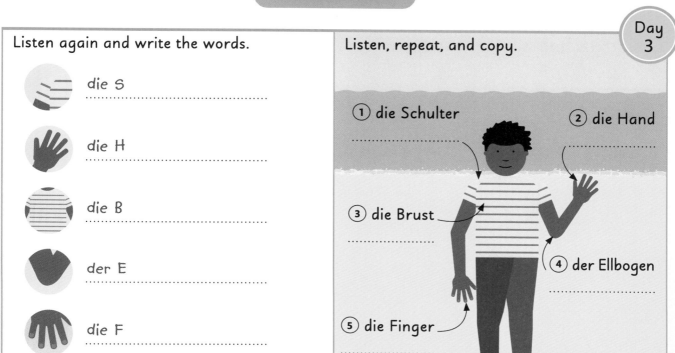

die S
....

die H
....

die B
....

der E
....

die F
....

Listen, repeat, and copy.

1 die Schulter
....

2 die Hand
....

3 die Brust
....

4 der Ellbogen
....

5 die Finger
....

Listen again and write the words.

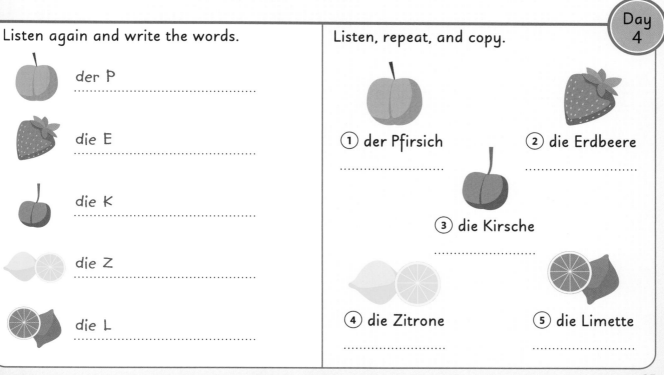

der P
....

die E
....

die K
....

die Z
....

die L
....

Listen, repeat, and copy.

1 der Pfirsich
....

2 die Erdbeere
....

3 die Kirsche
....

4 die Zitrone
....

5 die Limette
....

Day 5

What can you remember from this week?

1. Read the words and mark the correct pictures.

1 treffen

A ☐   B ☐

2 Schlittschuh laufen

A ☐   B ☐

3 Ski fahren

A ☐   B ☐

4 Fahrrad fahren

A ☐   B ☐

5 Skateboard fahren

A ☐   B ☐

2. Look at the pictures and fill in the missing letters.

1 d _ _   _ e _ f _ n

2 _ _ i _   Q _ a _ l _

3 d _ _   _ i _ t _ n _ i _ c _

4 _ _ e _   H _ _ i

5 d _ r   _ a _

3. Match the pictures to the correct words.

die Schulter

die Hand

die Finger

die Brust

der Ellbogen

4. Look at the pictures and write the correct words.

die Limette   die Kirsche   der Pfirsich
die Zitrone   die Erdbeere

1. die Z ....

2. die K ....

3. die E ....

4. der P ....

5. die L ....

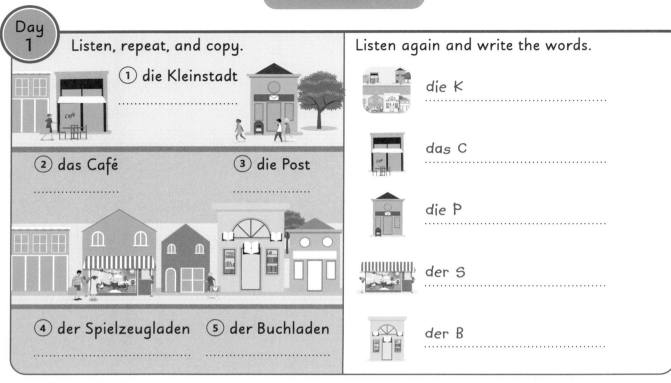

Day 1

Listen, repeat, and copy.

① die Kleinstadt

....

② das Café   ③ die Post

....

④ der Spielzeugladen   ⑤ der Buchladen

....

Listen again and write the words.

die K ....

das C ....

die P ....

der S ....

der B ....

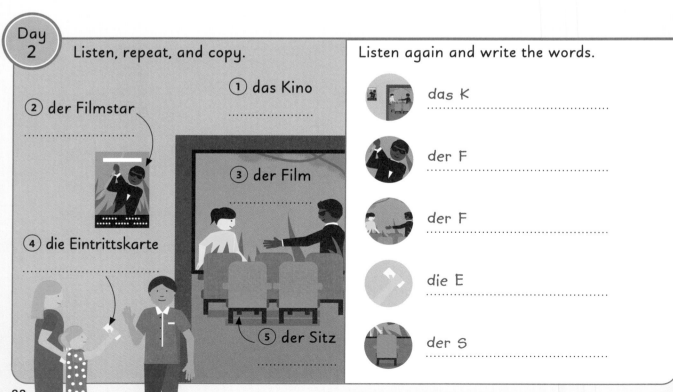

Day 2

Listen, repeat, and copy.

① das Kino

....

② der Filmstar

....

③ der Film

....

④ die Eintrittskarte

....

⑤ der Sitz

....

Listen again and write the words.

das K ....

der F ....

der F ....

die E ....

der S ....

Listen again and write the words.

das T ....

die E- ....

das E- ....

die N ....

die A ....

Listen, repeat, and copy.

① das Tablet
....

② die E-Mail
....

③ das E-Book
....

④ die Nachricht
....

⑤ die Apps
....

Listen again and write the words.

die S ....

die W ....

die R ....

die B ....

das F ....

Listen, repeat, and copy.

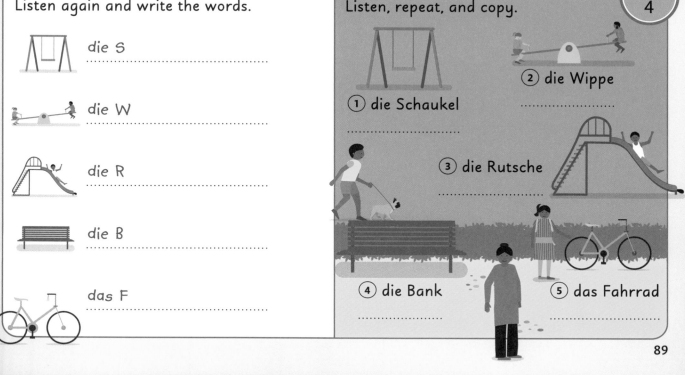

① die Schaukel
....

② die Wippe
....

③ die Rutsche
....

④ die Bank
....

⑤ das Fahrrad
....

Day 5

What can you remember from this week?

1. Look at the pictures and write the correct words.

1 das T ....

2 das E- ....

3 die N ....

4 die A ....

5 die E- ....

2. Match the pictures to the correct words.

1   die Post

2   das Café

3   der Buchladen

4   die Kleinstadt

5   der Spielzeugladen

3. Look at the pictures and circle the correct words.

der Sitz
das Kino

der Film
das Kino

der Filmstar
der Sitz

die Eintrittskarte
der Filmstar

die Eintrittskarte
der Film

4. Read the words and mark the correct pictures.

1 das Fahrrad

A ☐   B ☐

2 die Schaukel

A ☐   B ☐

3 die Bank

A ☐   B ☐

4 die Wippe

A ☐   B ☐

5 die Rutsche

A ☐   B ☐

Day 1

Listen, repeat, and copy.

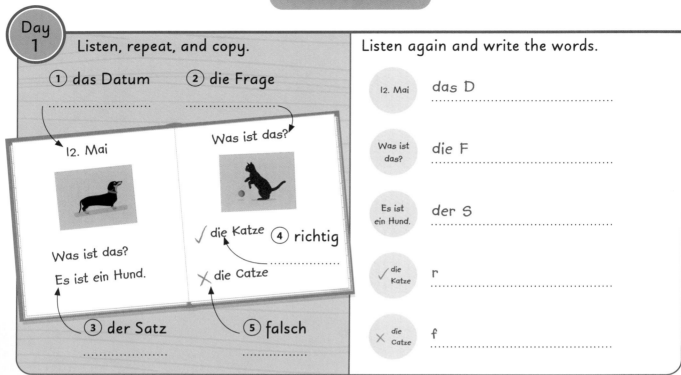

1. das Datum
....

2. die Frage
....

12. Mai

Was ist das?

Was ist das?

Es ist ein Hund.

✓ die Katze

✗ die Catze

3. der Satz
....

4. richtig

5. falsch
....

Listen again and write the words.

12. Mai — das D ....

Was ist das? — die F ....

Es ist ein Hund. — der S ....

✓ die Katze — r ....

✗ die Catze — f ....

Day 2

Listen, repeat, and copy.

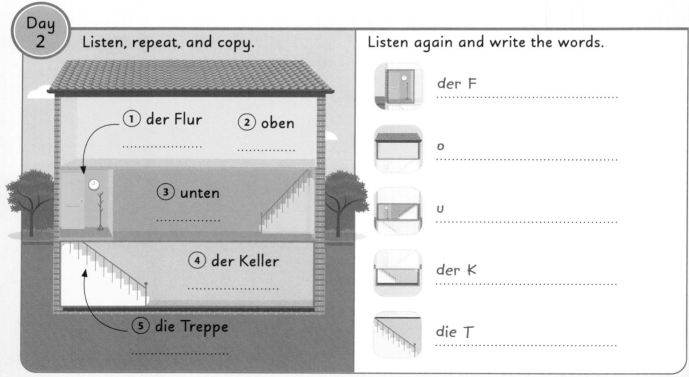

1. der Flur
....

2. oben
....

3. unten
....

4. der Keller
....

5. die Treppe
....

Listen again and write the words.

der F ....

o ....

U ....

der K ....

die T ....

Listen again and write the words.

 s ....

 s ....

 H ....

 a ....

 ü ....

Listen, repeat, and copy.

 ① saubermachen   ② sich entspannen

....

 ③ Hausaufgaben machen   ④ aufräumen

....

⑤ üben

....

Listen again and write the words.

 das S ....

 das S ....

 die S ....

 das H ....

 der B ....

Listen, repeat, and copy.

① das Schwimmbecken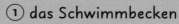

....

 ② das Schwimmen   ③ die Schwimmbrille

....

④ das Handtuch

....

⑤ der Badeanzug

....

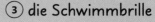 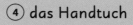 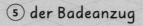 

93

Day 5

What can you remember from this week?

---

1. Look at the picture and write the correct words.

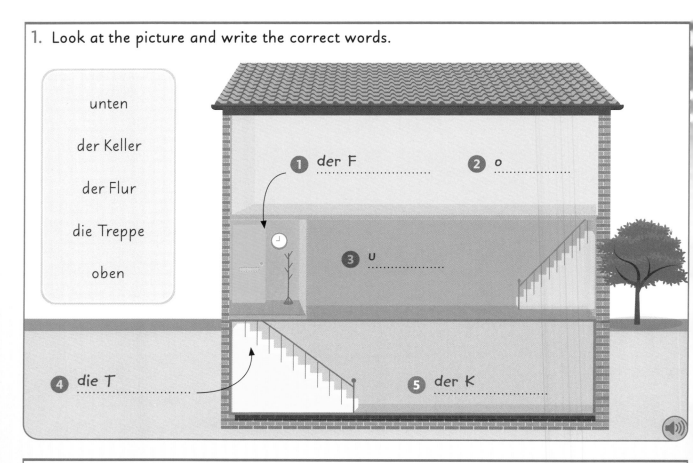

unten

der Keller

der Flur

die Treppe

oben

1 der F ....

2 o ....

3 u ....

4 die T ....

5 der K ....

---

2. Match the pictures to the correct words.

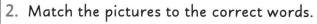

aufräumen   sich entspannen   Hausaufgaben machen   saubermachen   üben

3. Look at the pictures and circle the correct words.

das Schwimmbecken
das Handtuch

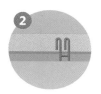

die Schwimmbrille
das Schwimmbecken

der Badeanzug
das Handtuch

die Schwimmbrille
das Schwimmen

das Schwimmen
der Badeanzug

4. Look at the pictures and fill in the missing letters.

✓ die Katze

_ i _ h _ i _

Was ist das?

d _ e _ _ _ r _ g _

12. Mai

_ a _ D _ t _ m

✗ die Catze

f _ l _ _ c _

Es ist ein Hund.

_ e _ S _ t _

Week 23

Day 1

Listen, repeat, and copy.

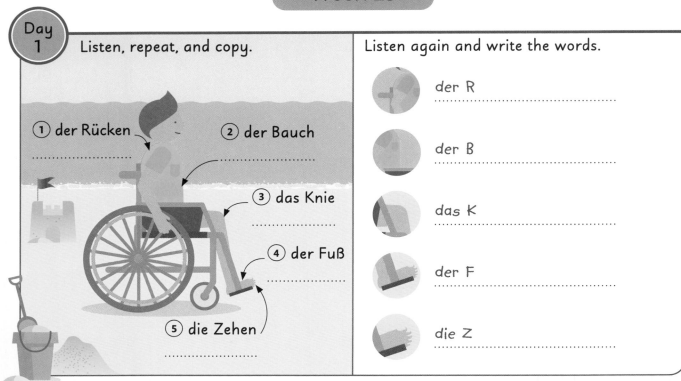

① der Rücken

② der Bauch

③ das Knie

④ der Fuß

⑤ die Zehen

Listen again and write the words.

der R

der B

das K

der F

die Z

Day 2

Listen, repeat, and copy.

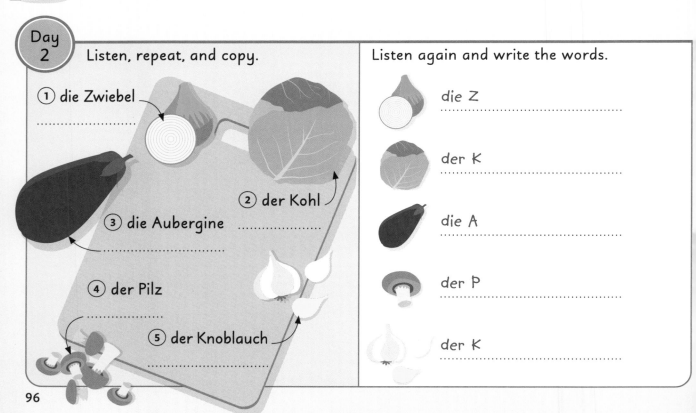

① die Zwiebel

② der Kohl

③ die Aubergine

④ der Pilz

⑤ der Knoblauch

Listen again and write the words.

die Z

der K

die A

der P

der K

96

Listen again and write the words.

G ....

V ....

T ....

F ....

T ....

Listen, repeat, and copy.

① Golf

② Volleyball

③ Tischtennis

④ Fußball

⑤ Turnen

Listen again and write the words.

der W ....

die H ....

der F ....

die E ....

die S ....

Listen, repeat, and copy.

① der Wasserfall

② die Höhle

③ der Fluss

④ die Eidechse

⑤ die Schildkröte

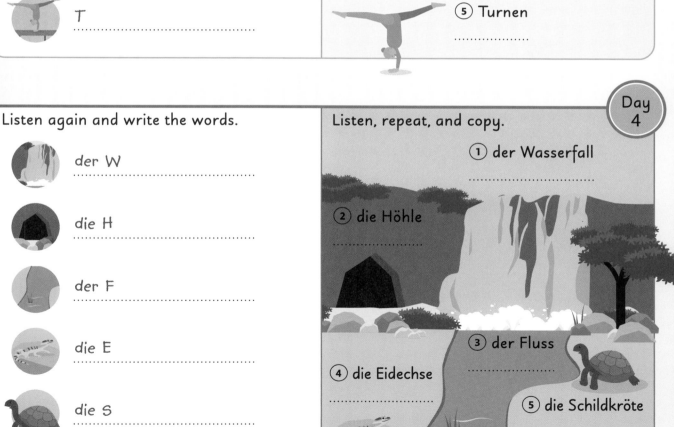

Day 5

What can you remember from this week?

1. Look at the pictures and mark the correct words.

① die Zwiebel ☐
der Kohl ☐

② der Pilz ☐
der Knoblauch ☐

③ der Kohl ☐
die Aubergine ☐

④ die Zwiebel ☐
der Pilz ☐

⑤ der Knoblauch ☐
die Aubergine ☐

2. Look at the pictures and write the correct words.

① der F ....

② der W ....

③ die H ....

④ die E ....

⑤ die S ....

3. Look at the pictures and circle the correct words.

 Golf / Turnen

 Volleyball / Fußball

 Tischtennis / Turnen

 Volleyball / Tischtennis

 Fußball / Golf

4. Look at the picture and write the correct words.

der Fuß

das Knie

der Bauch

der Rücken

die Zehen

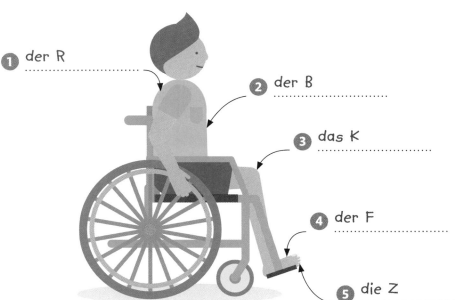

1 der R ....

2 der B ....

3 das K ....

4 der F ....

5 die Z ....

Day 1

Listen, repeat, and copy.

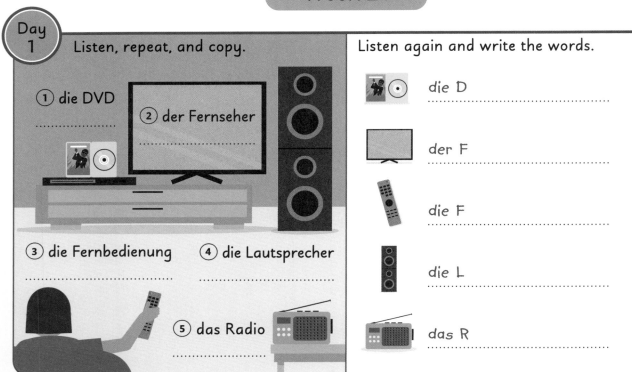

1. die DVD
2. der Fernseher
3. die Fernbedienung
4. die Lautsprecher
5. das Radio

Listen again and write the words.

die D ....

der F ....

die F ....

die L ....

das R ....

Day 2

Listen, repeat, and copy.

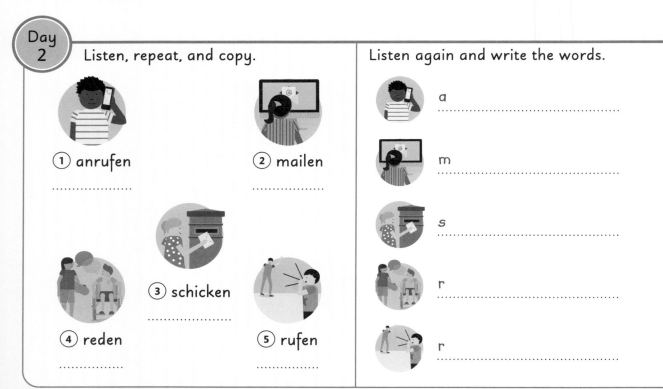

1. anrufen
2. mailen
3. schicken
4. reden
5. rufen

Listen again and write the words.

a ....

m ....

s ....

r ....

r ....

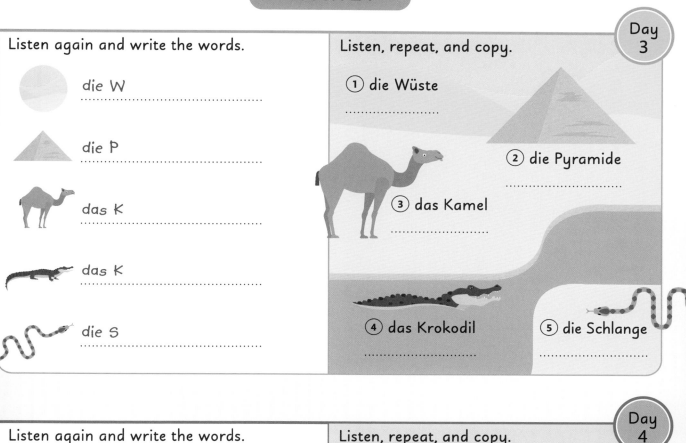

Day 3

Listen again and write the words.

die W ....

die P ....

das K ....

das K ....

die S ....

Listen, repeat, and copy.

① die Wüste
....

② die Pyramide
....

③ das Kamel
....

④ das Krokodil
....

⑤ die Schlange
....

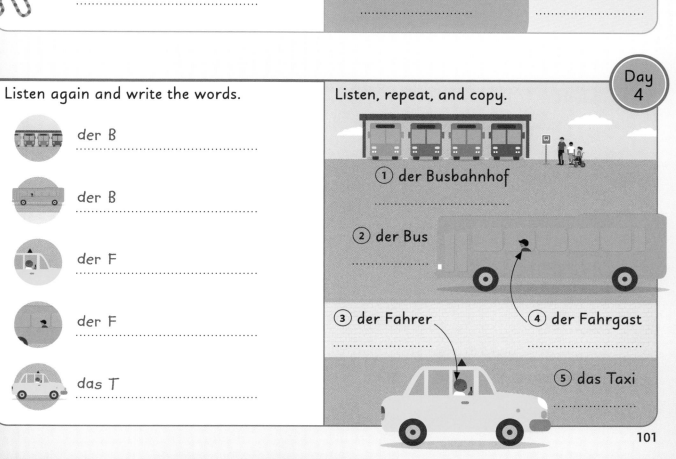

Day 4

Listen again and write the words.

der B ....

der B ....

der F ....

der F ....

das T ....

Listen, repeat, and copy.

① der Busbahnhof
....

② der Bus
....

③ der Fahrer
....

④ der Fahrgast
....

⑤ das Taxi
....

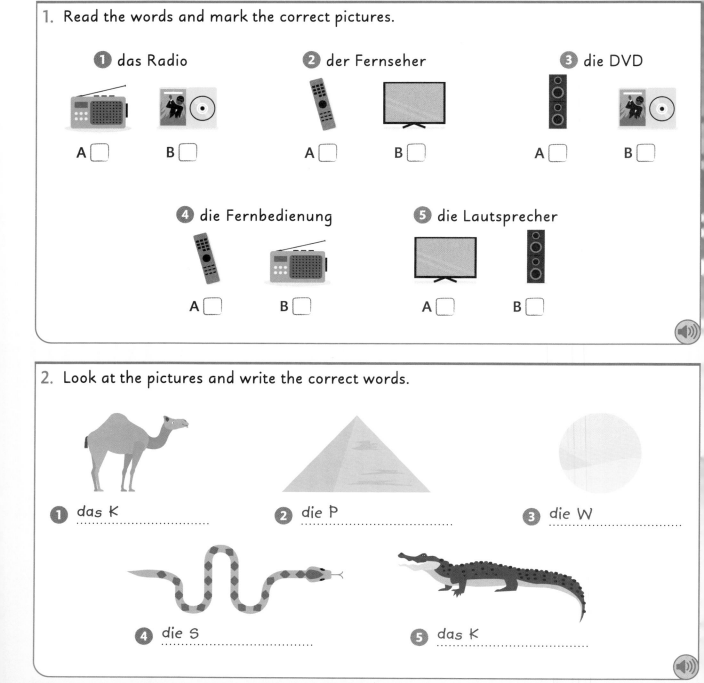

Day 5

What can you remember from this week?

1. Read the words and mark the correct pictures.

1 das Radio

A ☐   B ☐

2 der Fernseher

A ☐   B ☐

3 die DVD

A ☐   B ☐

4 die Fernbedienung

A ☐   B ☐

5 die Lautsprecher

A ☐   B ☐

2. Look at the pictures and write the correct words.

1 das K ....

2 die P ....

3 die W ....

4 die S ....

5 das K ....

Week 24

3. Match the pictures to the correct words.

der Fahrgast

das Taxi

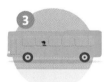

der Busbahnhof

der Bus

der Fahrer

4. Look at the pictures and circle the correct words.

schicken / anrufen

mailen / rufen

reden / schicken

anrufen / rufen

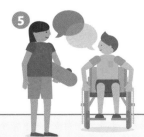

reden / mailen

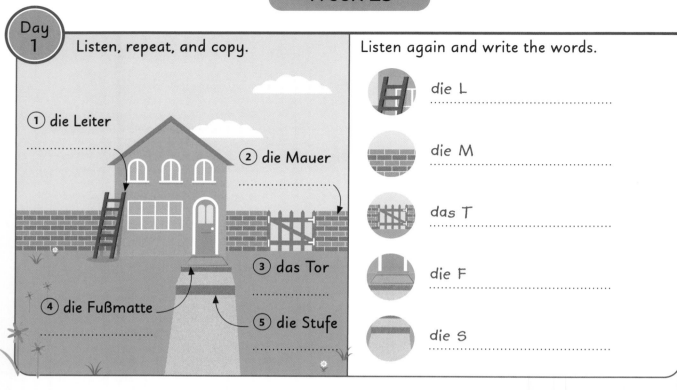

Day 1

Listen, repeat, and copy.

① die Leiter

② die Mauer

③ das Tor

④ die Fußmatte

⑤ die Stufe

Listen again and write the words.

die L

die M

das T

die F

die S

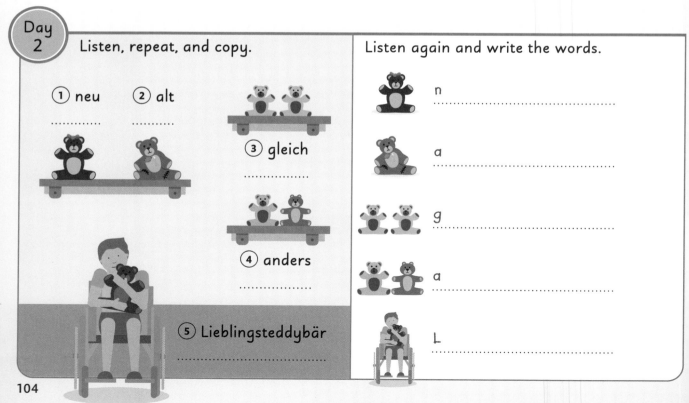

Day 2

Listen, repeat, and copy.

① neu

② alt

③ gleich

④ anders

⑤ Lieblingsteddybär

Listen again and write the words.

n

a

g

a

L

104

Listen again and write the words.

der K ....

der L ....

das M ....

das F ....

das A ....

Listen, repeat, and copy.

① der Krankenwagen ....

② der Lastwagen ....

③ das Motorrad ....

④ das Feuerwehrauto ....

⑤ das Auto ....

Listen again and write the words.

t ....

a ....

d ....

d ....

s ....

Listen, repeat, and copy.

① träumen ....

② aufwachen ....

③ das Bett machen ....

④ die Zähne putzen ....

⑤ sich anziehen ....

Day 5

What can you remember from this week?

1. Look at the pictures and write the correct words.

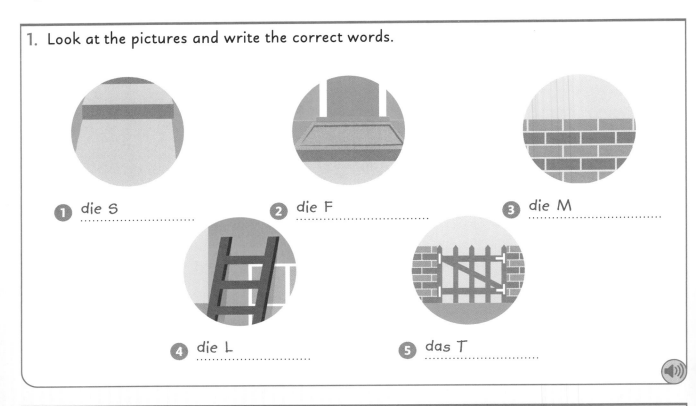

1 die S ....

2 die F ....

3 die M ....

4 die L ....

5 das T ....

2. Match the pictures to the correct words.

der Lastwagen   das Auto   der Krankenwagen   das Motorrad   das Feuerwehrauto

3. Read the words and mark
   the correct pictures.

1 aufwachen   A ☐   B ☐

2 das Bett
    machen   A ☐   B ☐

3 die Zähne
    putzen   A ☐   B ☐

4 sich anziehen   A ☐   B ☐

5 träumen   A ☐   B ☐

4. Look at the pictures and circle the
   correct words.

1 gleich
   Lieblingsteddybär

2 anders
   gleich

3 neu
   anders

4 alt
   Lieblingsteddybär

5 anders
   alt

Week 26

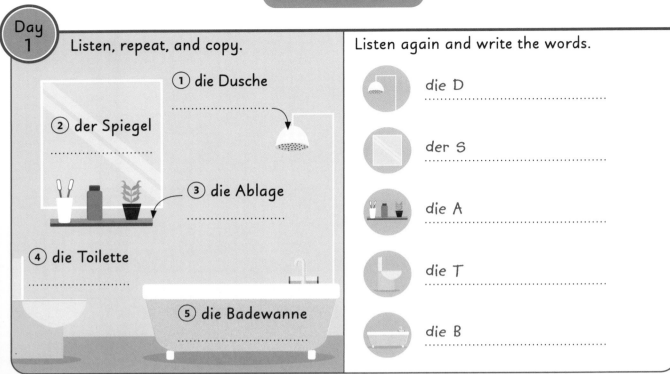

Listen, repeat, and copy.

① die Dusche

② der Spiegel

③ die Ablage

④ die Toilette

⑤ die Badewanne

Listen again and write the words.

die D ....

der S ....

die A ....

die T ....

die B ....

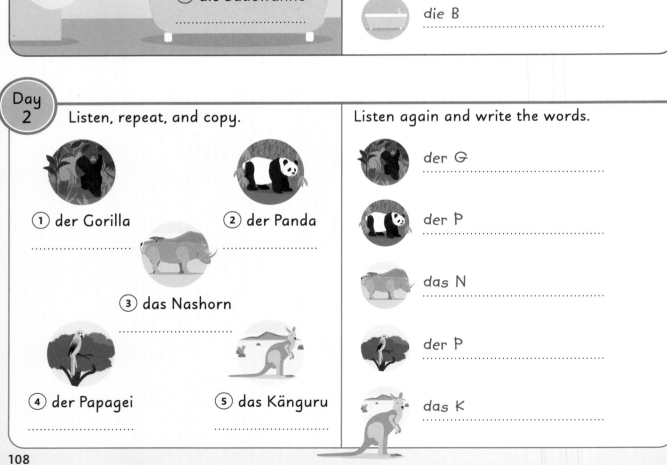

Listen, repeat, and copy.

① der Gorilla

② der Panda

③ das Nashorn

④ der Papagei

⑤ das Känguru

Listen again and write the words.

der G ....

der P ....

das N ....

der P ....

das K ....

Listen again and write the words.

u ....

s ....

w ....

h ....

e ....

Listen, repeat, and copy.

① umfallen
....

② sich wehtun
....

③ weinen
....

④ helfen
....

⑤ erzählen
....

Listen again and write the words.

der S ....

der M ....

der P ....

die H ....

die S ....

Listen, repeat, and copy.

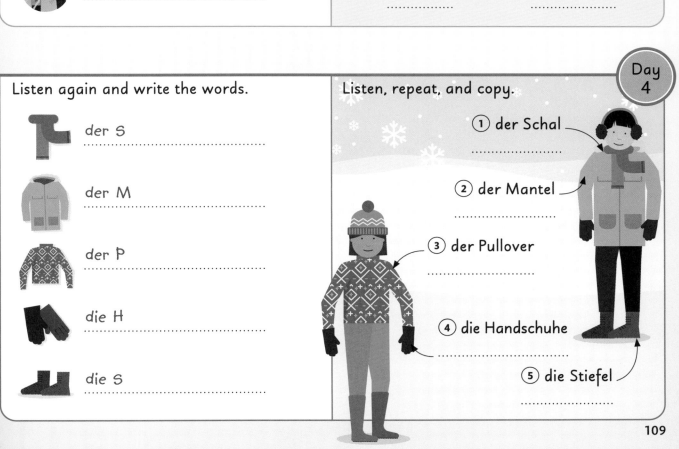

① der Schal
....

② der Mantel
....

③ der Pullover
....

④ die Handschuhe
....

⑤ die Stiefel
....

Day
5

What can you remember from this week?

1. Look at the pictures and write the correct words.

1 e ....

2 w ....

3 h ....

4 s ....

5 u ....

2. Look at the pictures and mark the correct words.

1
das Nashorn ☐
das Känguru ☐
der Papagei ☐

2
der Gorilla ☐
der Panda ☐
das Nashorn ☐

3
der Papagei ☐
das Nashorn ☐
der Gorilla ☐

4
das Känguru ☐
der Gorilla ☐
der Panda ☐

5
der Panda ☐
der Papagei ☐
das Känguru ☐

3. Look at the pictures and write the correct words.

der Mantel   die Stiefel   die Handschuhe   der Schal   der Pullover

1 die S ....

2 der P ....

3 der S ....

4 der M ....

5 die H ....

4. Look at the pictures and circle the correct words.

1 die Dusche
die Badewanne

2 die Toilette
die Ablage

3 die Badewanne
der Spiegel

4 der Spiegel
die Ablage

5 die Dusche
die Toilette

Week 27

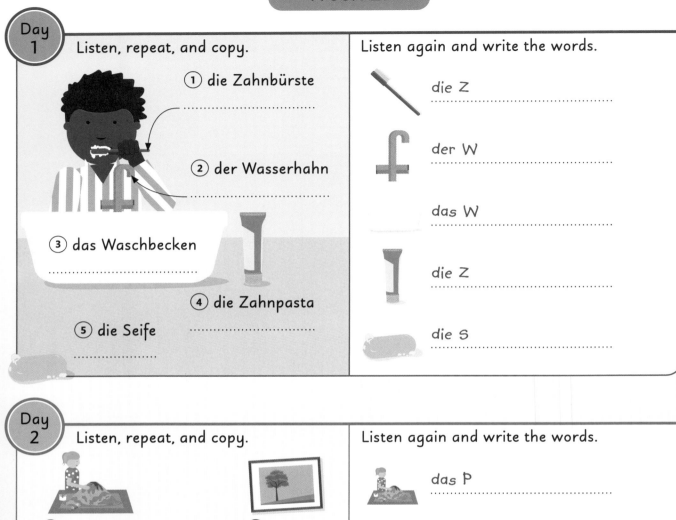

Day 1

Listen, repeat, and copy.

① die Zahnbürste

....

② der Wasserhahn

....

③ das Waschbecken

....

④ die Zahnpasta

⑤ die Seife ....

Listen again and write the words.

die Z ....

der W ....

das W ....

die Z ....

die S ....

Day 2

Listen, repeat, and copy.

① das Projekt

....

② das Bild

....

③ das Puzzle

....

④ die Geschichte

....

⑤ der Unterricht

....

Listen again and write the words.

das P ....

das B ....

das P ....

die G ....

der U ....

Listen again and write the words.

v ....

a ....

f ....

d ....

h ....

Listen, repeat, and copy.

(1) verängstigt ....

(2) aufgeregt ....

(3) freundlich ....

(4) durstig ....

(5) hungrig ....

Listen again and write the words.

der B ....

der S ....

die B ....

der W ....

das B ....

Listen, repeat, and copy.

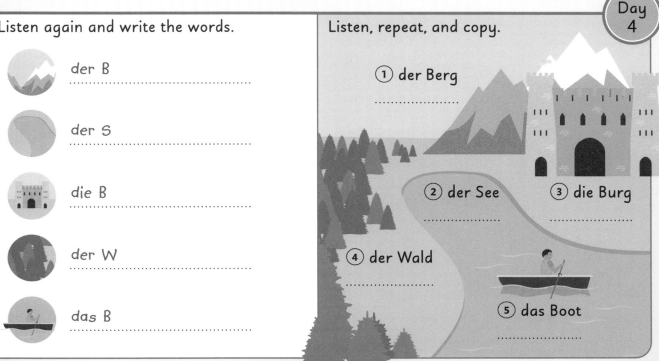

(1) der Berg ....

(2) der See ....

(3) die Burg ....

(4) der Wald ....

(5) das Boot ....

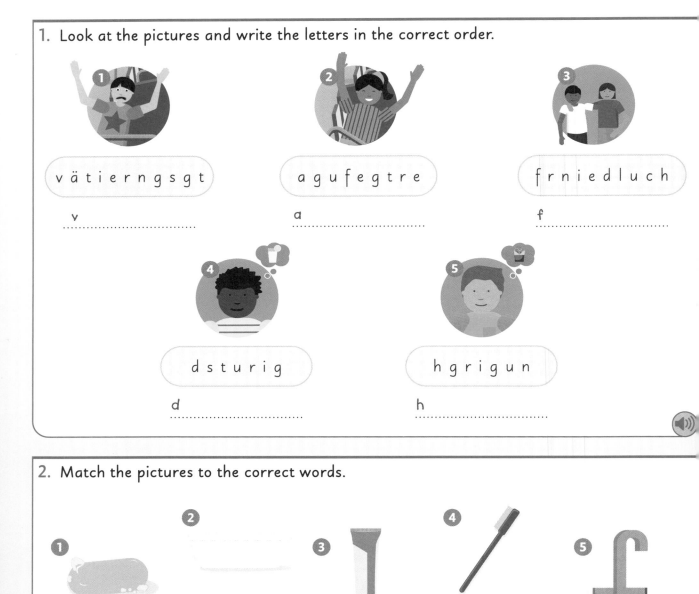

Day 5 What can you remember from this week?

1. Look at the pictures and write the letters in the correct order.

① v ä t i e r n g s g t

v ....

② a g u f e g t r e

a ....

③ f r n i e d l u c h

f ....

④ d s t u r i g

d ....

⑤ h g r i g u n

h ....

2. Match the pictures to the correct words.

① ② ③ ④ ⑤

die Zahnpasta   die Seife   das Waschbecken   der Wasserhahn   die Zahnbürste

3. Look at the pictures and mark the correct words.

 **1** das Projekt ☐
das Bild ☐

 **2** die Geschichte ☐
das Puzzle ☐

 **3** der Unterricht ☐
das Bild ☐

 **4** die Geschichte ☐
das Projekt ☐

 **5** das Puzzle ☐
der Unterricht ☐

4. Look at the pictures and fill in the missing letters.

 1 d _ r _ a _ d

 2 _ e _ B _ r _

 3 d _ e _ _ u _ g

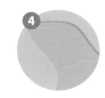 **4** _ e _ S _ e

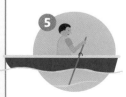 **5** d _ s _ o t

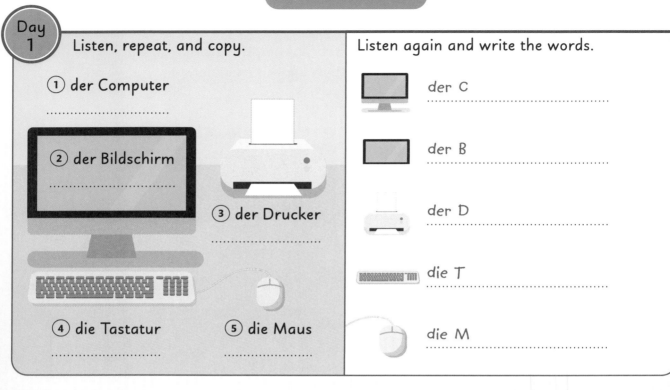

Day 1

Listen, repeat, and copy.

① der Computer

....

② der Bildschirm

....

③ der Drucker

....

④ die Tastatur

....

⑤ die Maus

....

Listen again and write the words.

der C

....

der B

....

der D

....

die T

....

die M

....

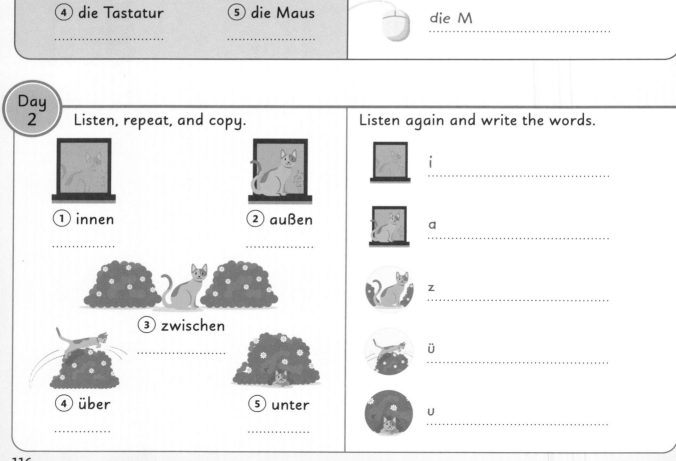

Day 2

Listen, repeat, and copy.

① innen

....

② außen

....

③ zwischen

....

④ über

....

⑤ unter

....

Listen again and write the words.

i

....

a

....

z

....

ü

....

u

....

Listen again and write the words.

 das W ....

 n ....

 b ....

 s ....

 w ....

Listen, repeat, and copy.

 ① das Wetter

....

 ② neblig

....

 ③ bewölkt

....

 ④ sonnig

....

⑤ windig

....

Listen again and write the words.

 der J ....

 der Z ....

 das F ....

 das E ....

 der C ....

Listen, repeat, and copy.

 ① der Jahrmarkt

....

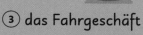

② der Zirkus   ③ das Fahrgeschäft

....

 ④ das Eis   ⑤ der Clown

....

Day 5

What can you remember from this week?

1. Read the words and mark the correct pictures.

① innen A ☐ B ☐

② außen A ☐ B ☐

③ zwischen A ☐ B ☐

④ über A ☐ B ☐

⑤ unter A ☐ B ☐

2. Look at the pictures and write the correct words.

1 n ....

2 s ....

3 das W ....

4 w ....

5 b ....

3. Look at the pictures and circle the correct words.

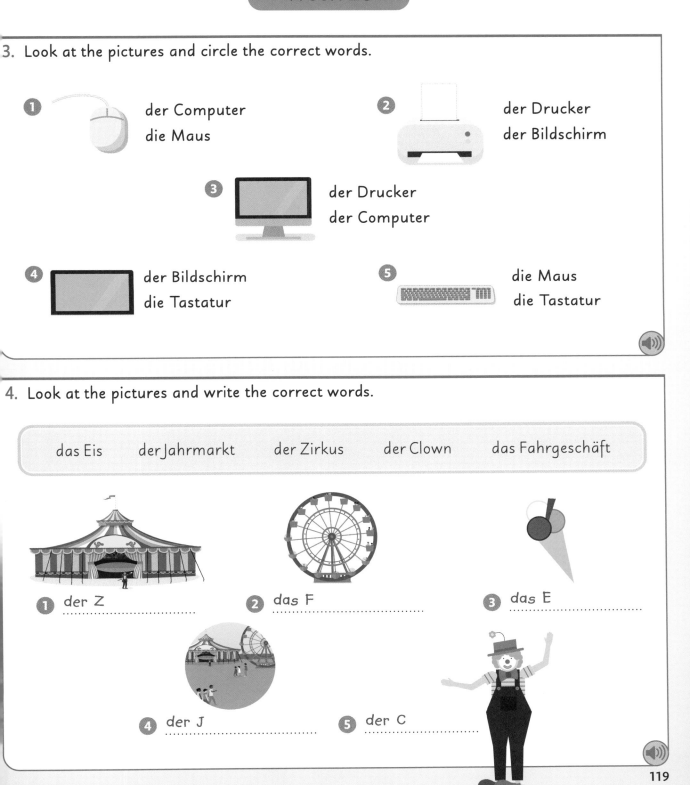

1. der Computer
   die Maus

2. der Drucker
   der Bildschirm

3. der Drucker
   der Computer

4. der Bildschirm
   die Tastatur

5. die Maus
   die Tastatur

4. Look at the pictures and write the correct words.

das Eis   der Jahrmarkt   der Zirkus   der Clown   das Fahrgeschäft

1. der Z

2. das F

3. das E

4. der J

5. der C

Week 29

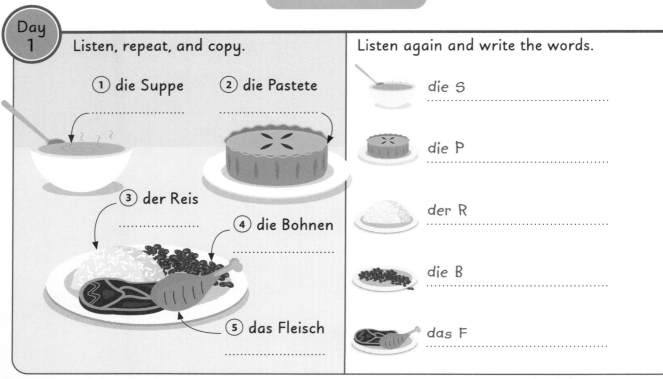

Day 1

Listen, repeat, and copy.

① die Suppe ② die Pastete

③ der Reis

④ die Bohnen

⑤ das Fleisch

Listen again and write the words.

die S

die P

der R

die B

das F

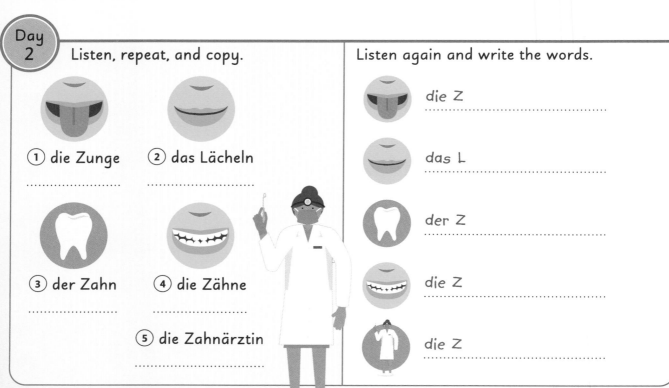

Day 2

Listen, repeat, and copy.

① die Zunge ② das Lächeln

③ der Zahn ④ die Zähne

⑤ die Zahnärztin

Listen again and write the words.

die Z

das L

der Z

die Z

die Z

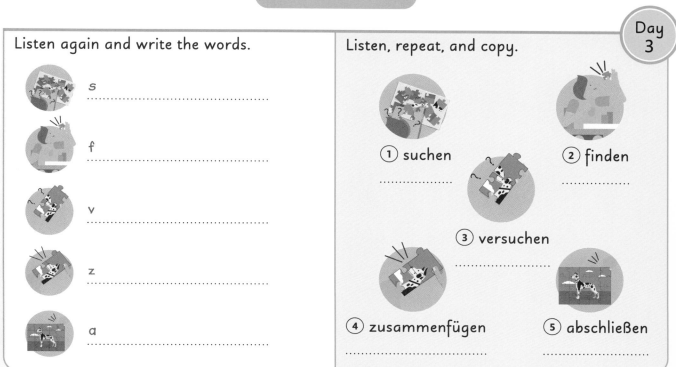

Day 3

Listen again and write the words.

s ....

f ....

v ....

z ....

a ....

Listen, repeat, and copy.

① suchen
....

② finden
....

③ versuchen
....

④ zusammenfügen
....

⑤ abschließen
....

Day 4

Listen again and write the words.

das F ....

die S ....

die A ....

der F ....

das N ....

Listen, repeat, and copy.

① das Fischen
....

② die Schwimmweste
....

③ die Angel
....

④ der Fisch
....

⑤ das Netz
....

Day 5

What can you remember from this week?

---

1. Look at the pictures and fill in the missing letters.

 s _ c _ e _

 f _ n _ e _

 z _ s _ m _ e _ f _ g _ n

 a _ s _ h _ i _ ß _ n

 v _ _ r _ u _ h _ n

---

2. Match the pictures to the correct words.

  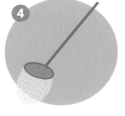 

das Fischen   der Fisch   die Schwimmweste   die Angel   das Netz

3. Look at the pictures and write the correct words.

1 die Z ....

2 die Z ....

3 der Z ....

4 das L ....

5 die Z ....

4. Look at the pictures and mark the correct words.

1
die Suppe ☐
die Bohnen ☐
der Reis ☐

2
das Fleisch ☐
die Pastete ☐
die Bohnen ☐

3
der Reis ☐
die Suppe ☐
die Pastete ☐

4
die Bohnen ☐
das Fleisch ☐
die Suppe ☐

5
die Pastete ☐
der Reis ☐
das Fleisch ☐

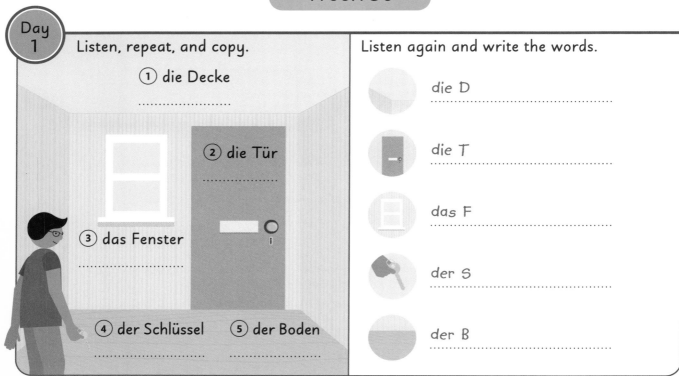

Day 1

Listen, repeat, and copy.

① die Decke

....

② die Tür

....

③ das Fenster

....

④ der Schlüssel

....

⑤ der Boden

....

Listen again and write the words.

die D ....

die T ....

das F ....

der S ....

der B ....

Day 2

Listen, repeat, and copy.

① die Erkältung

....

② die Kopfschmerzen

....

③ der Husten

....

④ die Bauchschmerzen

....

⑤ die Ohrenschmerzen

....

Listen again and write the words.

die E ....

die K ....

der H ....

die B ....

die O ....

Day 3

Listen again and write the words.

der B ....

die B ....

der U ....

der N ....

die A ....

Listen, repeat, and copy.

① der Brief
....

② die Briefmarke
....

③ der Umschlag
....

④ der Name
....

Sofia

Schulstraße 10
80636 München

⑤ die Adresse
....

Day 4

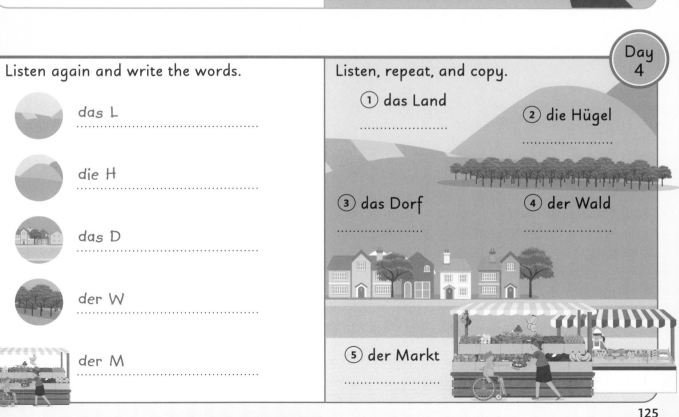

Listen again and write the words.

das L ....

die H ....

das D ....

der W ....

der M ....

Listen, repeat, and copy.

① das Land
....

② die Hügel
....

③ das Dorf
....

④ der Wald
....

⑤ der Markt
....

Day 5

What can you remember from this week?

1. Look at the pictures and write the correct words.

die Hügel   das Dorf   der Wald
das Land   der Markt

1. das D ....

2. die H ....

3. das L ....

4. der W ....

5. der M ....

2. Look at the pictures and mark the correct words.

1. der Brief ☐
   die Briefmarke ☐

2. Schulstraße 10
   80636 München
   der Name ☐
   die Adresse ☐

3. der Umschlag ☐
   der Brief ☐

4. die Adresse ☐
   die Briefmarke ☐

5. Sofia
   der Umschlag ☐
   der Name ☐

3. Read the words and mark the correct pictures.

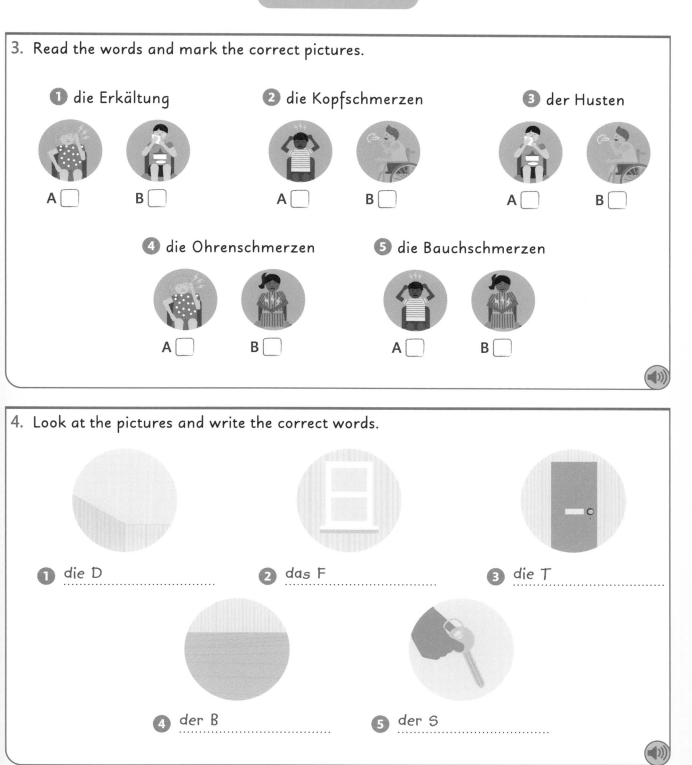

1 die Erkältung

A ☐   B ☐

2 die Kopfschmerzen

A ☐   B ☐

3 der Husten

A ☐   B ☐

4 die Ohrenschmerzen

A ☐   B ☐

5 die Bauchschmerzen

A ☐   B ☐

4. Look at the pictures and write the correct words.

1 die D ....

2 das F ....

3 die T ....

4 der B ....

5 der S ....

Week 31

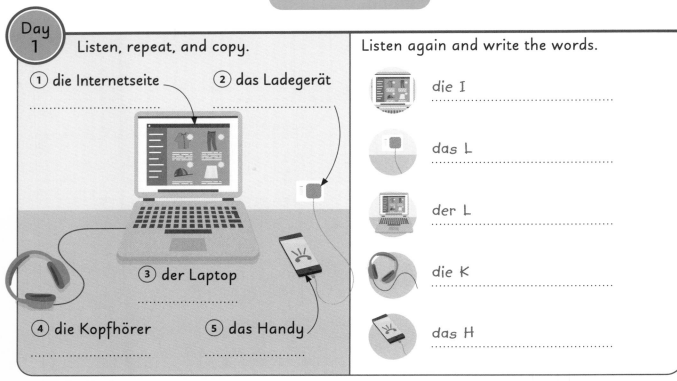

Day 1

Listen, repeat, and copy.

① die Internetseite

② das Ladegerät

③ der Laptop

④ die Kopfhörer

⑤ das Handy

Listen again and write the words.

die I

das L

der L

die K

das H

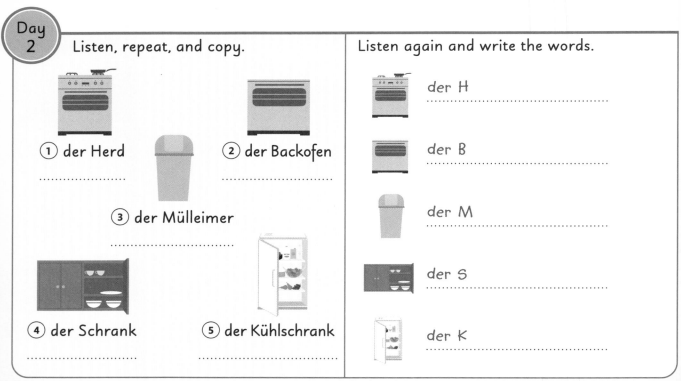

Day 2

Listen, repeat, and copy.

① der Herd

② der Backofen

③ der Mülleimer

④ der Schrank

⑤ der Kühlschrank

Listen again and write the words.

der H

der B

der M

der S

der K

128

Listen again and write the words.

das S
....

der S
....

das F
....

die B
....

das B
....

Listen, repeat, and copy.

① das Stadion
....

② der Supermarkt
....

③ das Fitnessstudio
....

④ die Bibliothek
....

⑤ das Büro
....

Listen again and write the words.

der H
....

die W
....

der B
....

der S
....

die I
....

Listen, repeat, and copy.

① der Himmel
....

② die Wolke
....

③ der Boden
....

④ der Stein
....

⑤ die Insekten
....

Day 5 — What can you remember from this week?

---

1. Read the words and mark the correct pictures.

1 der Laptop

A ☐ B ☐

2 die Internetseite

A ☐ B ☐

3 die Kopfhörer

A ☐ B ☐

4 das Handy

A ☐ B ☐

5 das Ladegerät

A ☐ B ☐

---

2. Look at the pictures and write the correct words.

1 das B ....

2 die B ....

3 das S ....

4 das F ....

5 der S ....

3. Look at the pictures and circle the correct words.

1 der Herd

der Schrank

2 der Mülleimer

der Herd

3 der Backofen

der Mülleimer

4 der Kühlschrank

der Schrank

5 der Backofen

der Kühlschrank

4. Look at the pictures and fill in the missing letters.

1 d _ r _ _ t i _

2 _ e _ H m e _

3 d _ e _ _ o k _

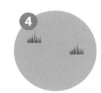

4 _ e _ B _ d _ n

5 d _ e _ _ n _ e t n

Week 32

Day 1

Listen, repeat, and copy.

① die Schneeflocke

....

② der Schneemann

....

③ der Schneeball

....

④ der Schnee   ⑤ das Eis

....

Listen again and write the words.

die S ....

der S ....

der S ....

der S ....

das E ....

Day 2

Listen, repeat, and copy.

① hüpfen

....

② drehen

....

③ schaukeln

....

④ spielen

....

⑤ pfeifen

....

Listen again and write the words.

h ....

d ....

s ....

s ....

p ....

132

Week 32

Listen again and write the words.

 die S ....

 die B ....

 der V ....

 der Z ....

 die A ....

Day 3

Listen, repeat, and copy.

 ① die Straße
....

 ② die Bushaltestelle
....

 ③ der Verkehr
....

 ④ der Zebrastreifen
....

 ⑤ die Ampel

Listen again and write the words.

 das R ....

 die K ....

 das E ....

 die S ....

 die K ....

Day 4

Listen, repeat, and copy.

 ① das Restaurant
....

② die Köchin
....

③ das Essen

④ die Speisekarte
....

 ⑤ die Kellnerin
....

133

Day 5

What can you remember from this week?

1. Read the words and mark the correct pictures.

1 der Schneemann   A ☐   B ☐

2 der Schnee   A ☐   B ☐

3 die Schneeflocke   A ☐   B ☐

4 der Schneeball   A ☐   B ☐

5 das Eis   A ☐   B ☐

2. Look at the pictures and write the correct words.

1 die S ....

2 das R ....

3 die K ....

4 das E ....

5 die K ....

3. Look at the pictures and write the letters in the correct order.

slepeni

1 s _ _ _ _ _ _

hpnfüe

2 h _ _ _ _ _

dhenre

3 d _ _ _ _ _

skelchaun

4 s _ _ _ _ _ _ _ _

pffneie

5 p _ _ _ _ _ _

4. Match the pictures to the correct words.

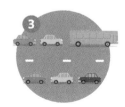

der Verkehr   der Zebrastreifen   die Straße   die Ampel   die Bushaltestelle

Day 1

Listen, repeat, and copy.

① die Tasse

② der Teller

③ die Schüssel

④ das Glas

⑤ die Flasche

Listen again and write the words.

die T ....

der T ....

die S ....

das G ....

die F ....

Day 2

Listen, repeat, and copy.

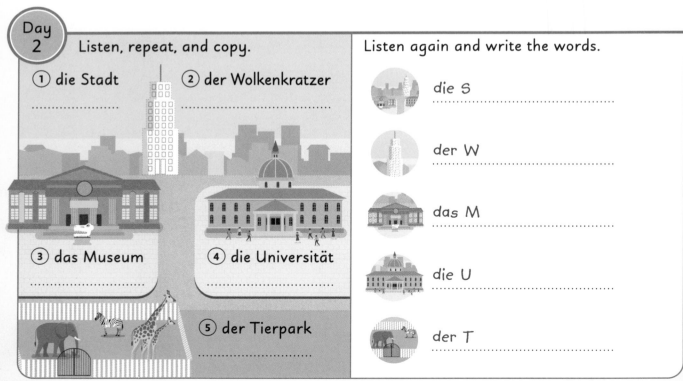

① die Stadt

② der Wolkenkratzer

③ das Museum

④ die Universität

⑤ der Tierpark

Listen again and write the words.

die S ....

der W ....

das M ....

die U ....

der T ....

Listen again and write the words.

s ....

a ....

e ....

b ....

f ....

Listen, repeat, and copy.

① starten
....

② ansehen
....

③ ein Wettrennen machen
....

④ beenden
....

⑤ filmen
....

Listen again and write the words.

der G ....

das G ....

der E ....

der K ....

der E ....

Listen, repeat, and copy.

① der Geldbeutel
....

② das Geld
....

③ der Einkaufswagen
....

④ der Korb
....

⑤ der Einkauf
....

Day 5 What can you remember from this week?

1. Look at the pictures and fill in the missing letters.

① d _ r _ e _ l _ r

② d _ e _ _ _ s _ h _

③ d _ s _ _ l _ s

④ d _ e _ c _ ü _ s _ l

⑤ d _ e _ _ a _ s _

2. Read the words and mark the correct pictures.

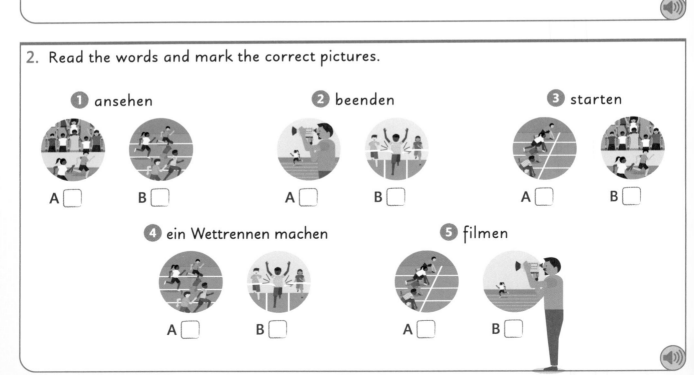

① ansehen   A ☐   B ☐

② beenden   A ☐   B ☐

③ starten   A ☐   B ☐

④ ein Wettrennen machen   A ☐   B ☐

⑤ filmen   A ☐   B ☐

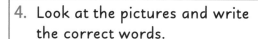

Week 33

3. Look at the pictures and circle the correct words.

das Geld
der Geldbeutel

der Einkauf
der Korb

der Korb
der Einkaufswagen

der Einkauf
das Geld

der Geldbeutel
der Einkaufswagen

4. Look at the pictures and write the correct words.

der T ....

die S ....

das M ....

die U ....

der W ....

Day 1

Listen, repeat, and copy.

① das Picknick

② der Weg

③ die Decke

④ die Brücke

⑤ der Bach

Listen again and write the words.

das P

der W

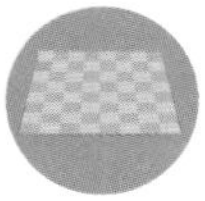

die D

die B

der B

Day 2

Listen, repeat, and copy.

① die Führung

② die Aussicht

③ das Foto

④ die Postkarte

⑤ der Fotoapparat

Listen again and write the words.

die F

die A

das F

die P

der F

Listen again and write the words.

a ....

r ....

t ....

s ....

z ....

Listen, repeat, and copy.

① arbeiten ....

② reisen ....

③ treffen ....

④ sprechen ....

⑤ zeigen ....

Listen again and write the words.

die S ....

der M ....

die E ....

die R ....

die A ....

Listen, repeat, and copy.

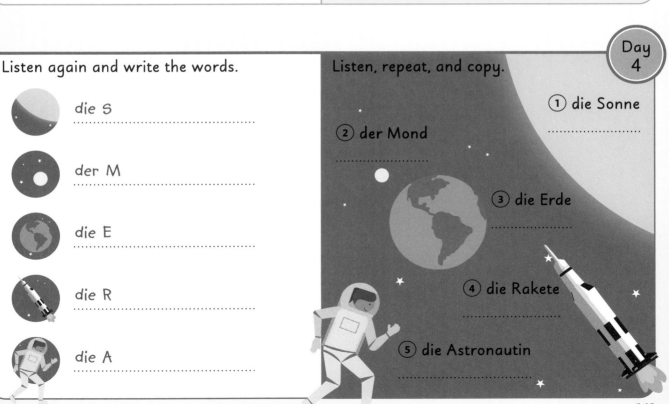

① die Sonne ....

② der Mond ....

③ die Erde ....

④ die Rakete ....

⑤ die Astronautin

Day 5

What can you remember from this week?

1. Look at the pictures and write the letters in the correct order.

1. r s e n e i

r _ _ _ _ _ _

2. a e i n r b t e

a _ _ _ _ _ _ _

3. s p h e n r e c

s _ _ _ _ _ _ _

4. t r n f e e f

t _ _ _ _ _ _

5. z g e e i n

z _ _ _ _ _ _

2. Look at the pictures and mark the correct words.

1. die Sonne ☐
   die Astronautin ☐
   der Mond ☐

2. die Rakete ☐
   die Erde ☐
   die Astronautin ☐

3. die Sonne ☐
   der Mond ☐
   die Erde ☐

4. der Mond ☐
   die Rakete ☐
   die Astronautin ☐

5. die Sonne ☐
   die Erde ☐
   die Rakete ☐

3. Look at the pictures and write the correct words.

der Weg   die Brücke   das Picknick   der Bach   die Decke

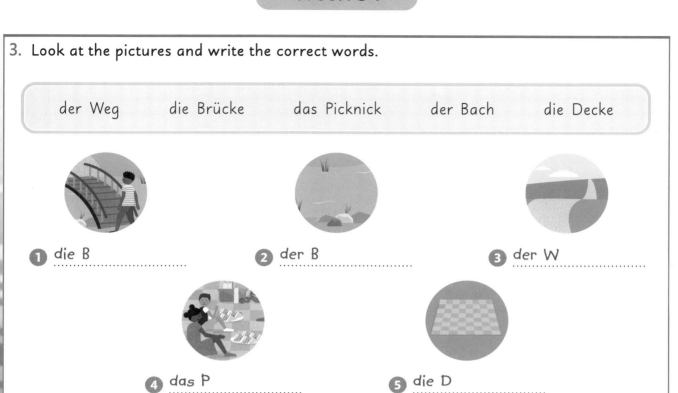

1 die B ....

2 der B ....

3 der W ....

4 das P ....

5 die D ....

4. Look at the pictures and circle the correct words.

1 das Foto
der Fotoapparat

2 die Postkarte
die Aussicht

3 die Führung
der Fotoapparat

4 die Führung
die Aussicht

5 das Foto
die Postkarte

Day 1

Listen, repeat, and copy.

① oben

② in der Mitte

③ unten

④ klein

⑤ groß

Listen again and write the words.

o ....

i ....

u ....

k ....

g ....

Day 2

Listen, repeat, and copy.

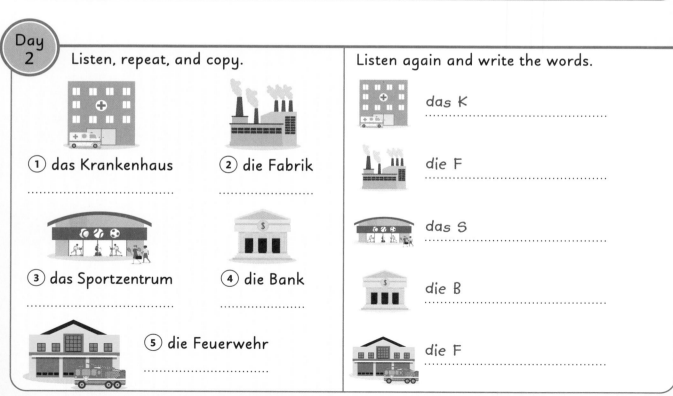

① das Krankenhaus

② die Fabrik

③ das Sportzentrum

④ die Bank

⑤ die Feuerwehr

Listen again and write the words.

das K ....

die F ....

das S ....

die B ....

die F ....

Listen again and write the words.

n ....

t ....

w ....

h ....

k ....

Listen, repeat, and copy.

① nass

② trocken

③ warm

④ heiß

⑤ kalt

Listen again and write the words.

l ....

f ....

s ....

l ....

l ....

Listen, repeat, and copy.

① leihen

② flüstern

③ suchen

④ lernen

⑤ lesen

Day 5

What can you remember from this week?

1. Read the words and mark the correct pictures.

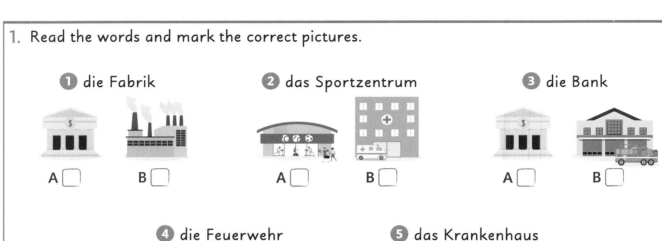

1 die Fabrik

A ☐ B ☐

2 das Sportzentrum

A ☐ B ☐

3 die Bank

A ☐ B ☐

4 die Feuerwehr

A ☐ B ☐

5 das Krankenhaus

A ☐ B ☐

2. Look at the pictures and fill in the missing letters.

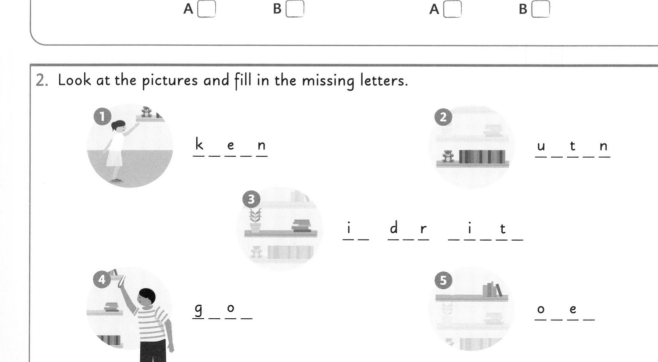

1 k _ e _ _ n

2 u _ _ t _ n

3 i_ _ d _ _ r _ _ _ _ i _ t _

4 g _ _ o _

5 o _ e _

3. Look at the pictures and write the correct words.

w ....

t ....

n ....

k ....

h ....

4. Match the pictures to the correct words.

flüstern

lernen

leihen

suchen

lesen

Week 36

Day 1

Listen, repeat, and copy.

① der Tee

② die Milch

③ der Zucker

④ der Kaffee ⑤ der Keks

Listen again and write the words.

der T

die M

der Z

der K

der K

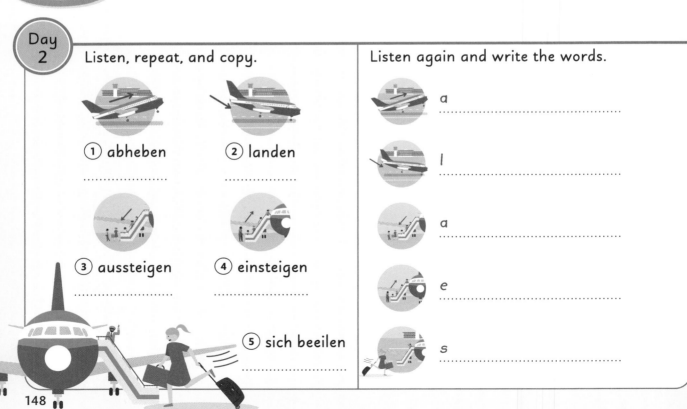

Day 2

Listen, repeat, and copy.

① abheben ② landen

③ aussteigen ④ einsteigen

⑤ sich beeilen

Listen again and write the words.

a

l

a

e

s

148

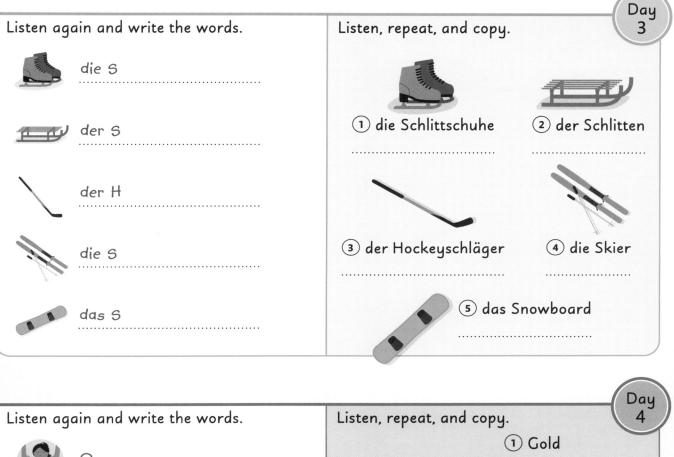

Listen again and write the words.

die S ....

der S ....

der H ....

die S ....

das S ....

Listen, repeat, and copy.

① die Schlittschuhe ....

② der Schlitten ....

③ der Hockeyschläger ....

④ die Skier ....

⑤ das Snowboard ....

Listen again and write the words.

G ....

S ....

B ....

das R ....

der G ....

Listen, repeat, and copy.

① Gold ....

② Silber ....

③ Bronze ....

④ das Rennen ....

⑤ der Gewinner ....

Day 5

What can you remember from this week?

1. Look at the pictures and write the correct words.

die Milch   der Tee   der Kaffee
der Zucker   der Keks

1. der T ....

2. der K ....

3. der K ....

4. die M ....

5. der Z ....

2. Look at the pictures and circle the correct words.

1. das Rennen
   Gold

2. Silber
   der Gewinner

3. Silber
   Gold

4. der Gewinner
   Bronze

5. das Rennen
   Bronze

3. Look at the pictures and fill in the missing letters.

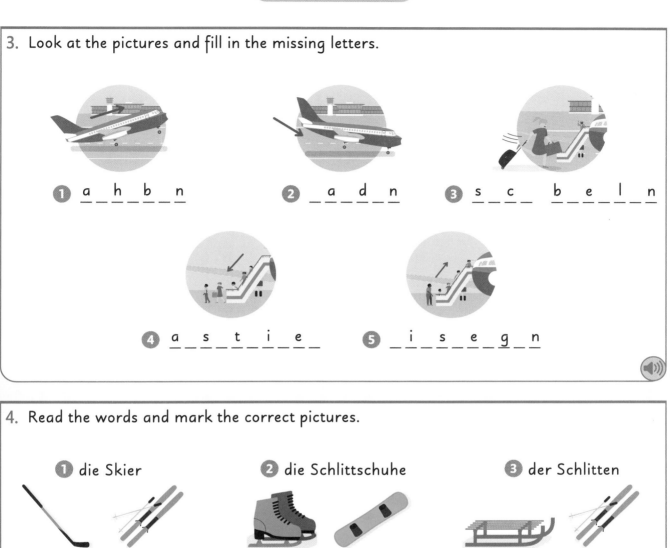

1 <u>a</u> <u>_</u> <u>h</u> <u>_</u> <u>b</u> <u>_</u> <u>n</u>

2 <u>_</u> <u>a</u> <u>_</u> <u>d</u> <u>_</u> <u>n</u>

3 <u>s</u> <u>_</u> <u>c</u> <u>_</u> <u>b</u> <u>e</u> <u>_</u> <u>l</u> <u>_</u> <u>n</u>

4 <u>a</u> <u>_</u> <u>s</u> <u>_</u> <u>t</u> <u>_</u> <u>i</u> <u>e</u> <u>_</u>

5 <u>_</u> <u>i</u> <u>_</u> <u>s</u> <u>e</u> <u>_</u> <u>g</u> <u>_</u> <u>n</u>

4. Read the words and mark the correct pictures.

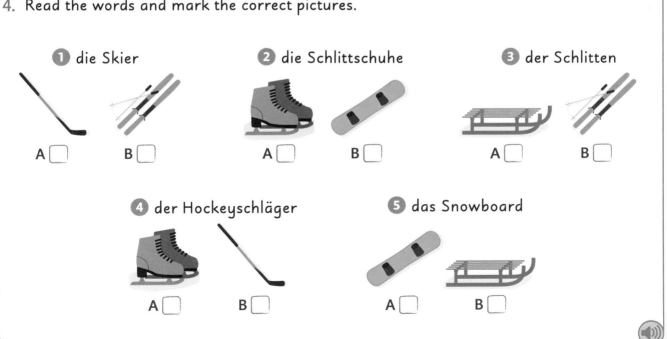

1 die Skier

A ☐   B ☐

2 die Schlittschuhe

A ☐   B ☐

3 der Schlitten

A ☐   B ☐

4 der Hockeyschläger

A ☐   B ☐

5 das Snowboard

A ☐   B ☐

151

Day 1

Listen, repeat, and copy.

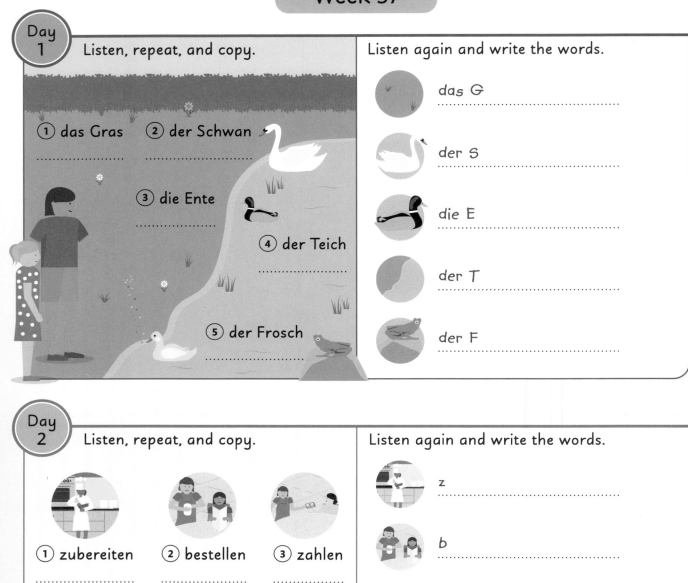

① das Gras   ② der Schwan

③ die Ente

④ der Teich

⑤ der Frosch

Listen again and write the words.

das G

der S

die E

der T

der F

Day 2

Listen, repeat, and copy.

① zubereiten   ② bestellen   ③ zahlen

④ mögen   ⑤ nicht mögen

Listen again and write the words.

z

b

z

m

n

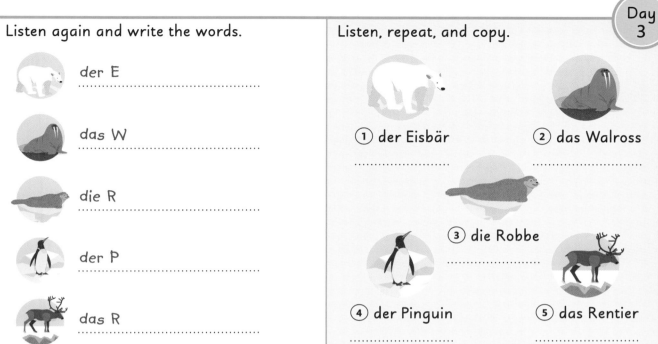

Listen again and write the words.

der E
....

das W
....

die R
....

der P
....

das R
....

Listen, repeat, and copy.

① der Eisbär

② das Walross
....

③ die Robbe
....

④ der Pinguin
....

⑤ das Rentier
....

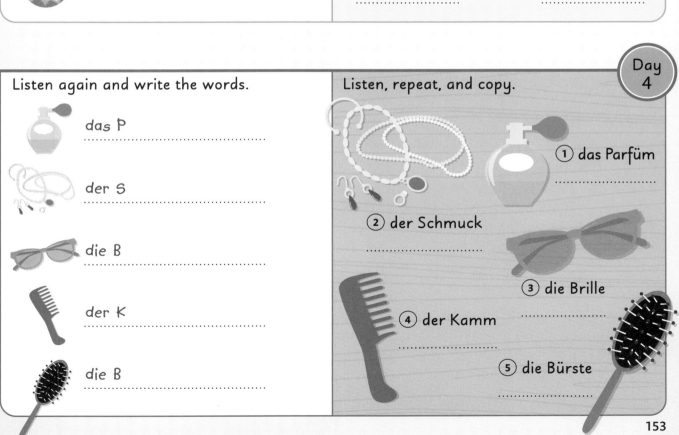

Listen again and write the words.

das P
....

der S
....

die B
....

der K
....

die B
....

Listen, repeat, and copy.

① das Parfüm
....

② der Schmuck
....

③ die Brille
....

④ der Kamm
....

⑤ die Bürste
....

Day 5

What can you remember from this week?

---

1. Look at the pictures and write the correct words.

| zahlen | nicht mögen | mögen | bestellen | zubereiten |

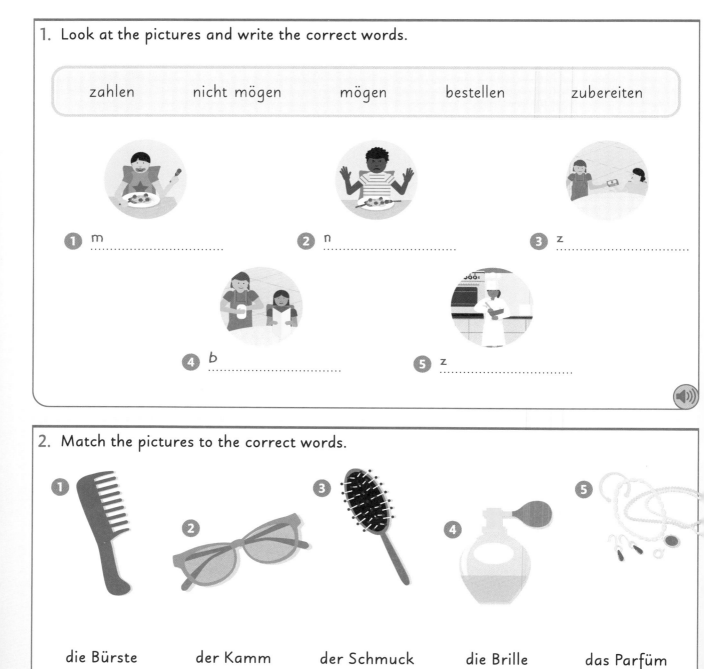

1 m ....

2 n ....

3 z ....

4 b ....

5 z ....

---

2. Match the pictures to the correct words.

1

2

3

4

5

die Bürste   der Kamm   der Schmuck   die Brille   das Parfüm

3. Look at the pictures and mark
   the correct words.

1. der Pinguin ☐
   das Walross ☐

2. der Eisbär ☐
   der Pinguin ☐

3. das Rentier ☐
   die Robbe ☐

4. das Rentier ☐
   der Eisbär ☐

5. die Robbe ☐
   das Walross ☐

4. Look at the pictures and write
   the correct words.

1. das G ....

2. der F ....

3. der T ....

4. der S ....

5. die E ....

Day 1

Listen, repeat, and copy.

① der Salat

② die Tomate   ③ der Käse

④ die Oliven   ⑤ der Kopfsalat

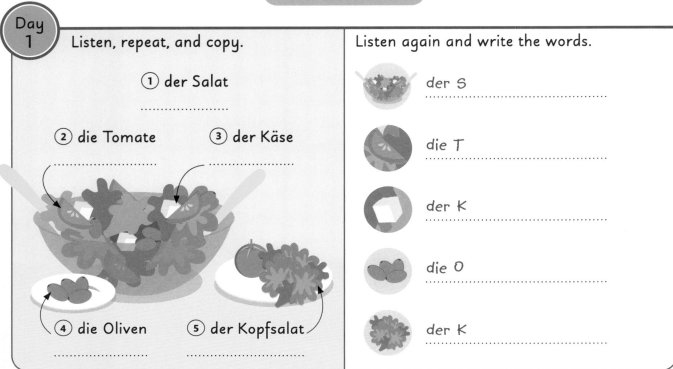

Listen again and write the words.

der S

die T

der K

die O

der K

Day 2

Listen, repeat, and copy.

① braunhaarig   ② blond

③ schwarzhaarig

④ grauhaarig   ⑤ rothaarig

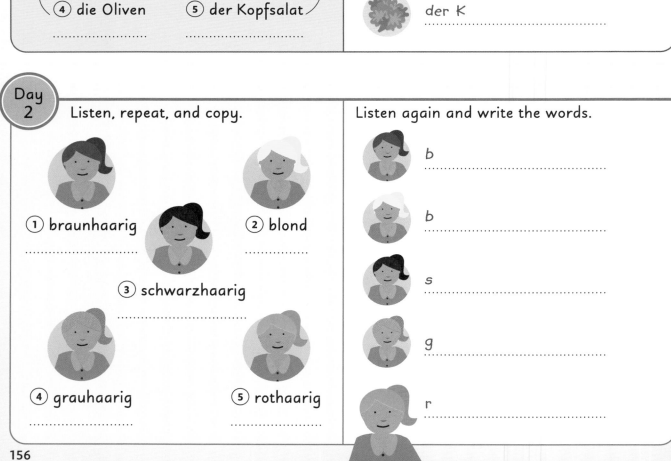

Listen again and write the words.

b

b

s

g

r

Listen again and write the words.

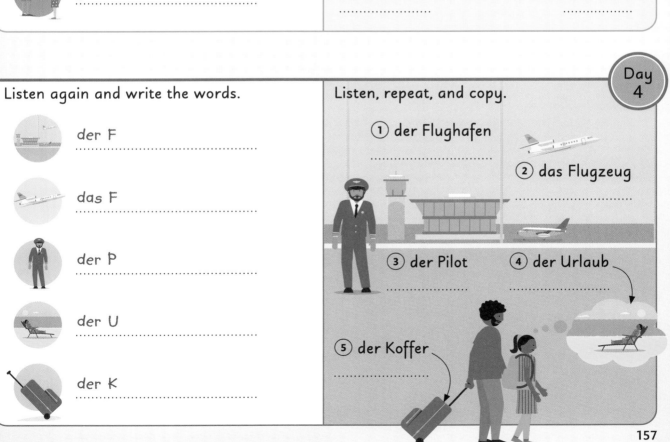

a ....

b ....

m ....

b ....

g ....

Listen, repeat, and copy.

① ankommen
....

② begrüßen
....

③ mitbringen
....

④ besuchen
....

⑤ geben
....

Listen again and write the words.

der F ....

das F ....

der P ....

der U ....

der K ....

Listen, repeat, and copy.

① der Flughafen
....

② das Flugzeug
....

③ der Pilot
....

④ der Urlaub
....

⑤ der Koffer
....

Day 5

What can you remember from this week?

1. Look at the pictures and mark the correct words.

1
- das Flugzeug ☐
- der Pilot ☐
- der Urlaub ☐

2
- der Koffer ☐
- das Flugzeug ☐
- der Flughafen ☐

3
- der Urlaub ☐
- der Koffer ☐
- der Pilot ☐

4
- der Urlaub ☐
- der Koffer ☐
- der Flughafen ☐

5
- der Pilot ☐
- der Flughafen ☐
- das Flugzeug ☐

2. Look at the pictures and write the letters in the correct order.

1 m b g e r i n i t n

m _ _ _ _ _ _ _ _ _

2 a m m o e n k n

a _ _ _ _ _ _ _

3 b s h u e n c e

b _ _ _ _ _ _ _

4 g e e n b

g _ _ _ _

5 b e n ß ü g r e

b _ _ _ _ _ _ _

3. Look at the pictures and write the correct words.

grauhaarig   blond   schwarzhaarig   rothaarig   braunhaarig

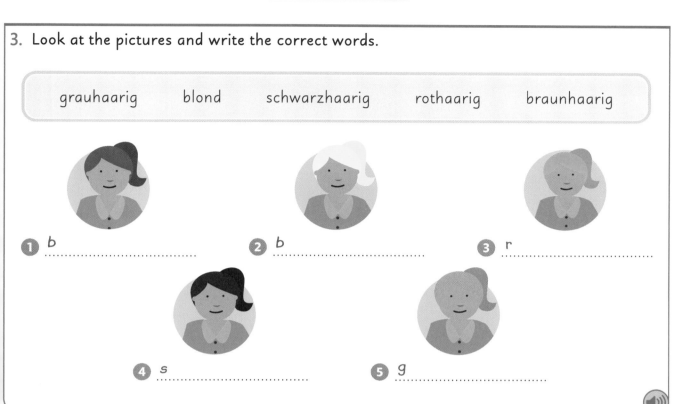

1 b ....

2 b ....

3 r ....

4 s ....

5 g ....

4. Look at the picture and write the correct words.

die Oliven

der Käse

der Salat

die Tomate

der Kopfsalat

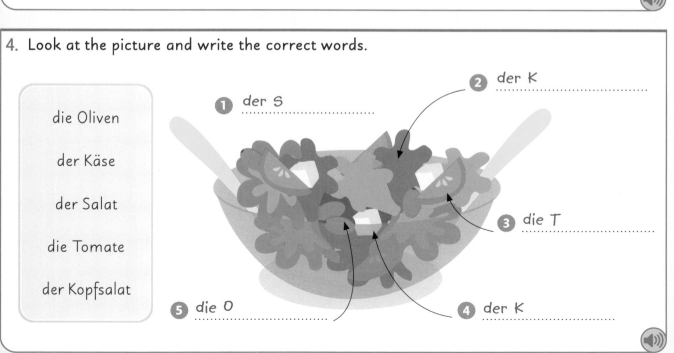

1 der S ....

2 der K ....

3 die T ....

4 der K ....

5 die O ....

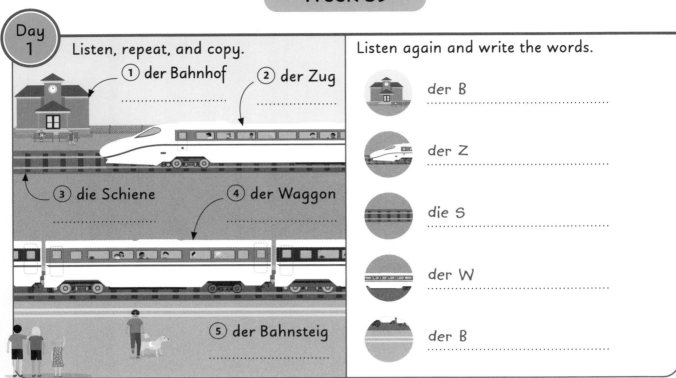

Day 1

Listen, repeat, and copy.

① der Bahnhof ② der Zug

....

③ die Schiene ④ der Waggon

....

⑤ der Bahnsteig

....

Listen again and write the words.

der B ....

der Z ....

die S ....

der W ....

der B ....

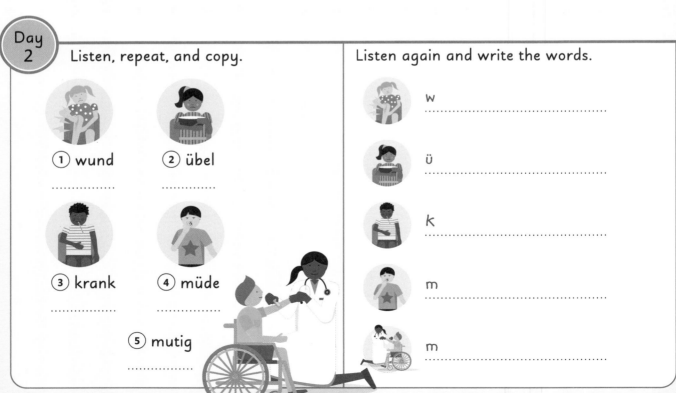

Day 2

Listen, repeat, and copy.

① wund ② übel

....

③ krank ④ müde

....

⑤ mutig

....

Listen again and write the words.

w ....

ü ....

k ....

m ....

m ....

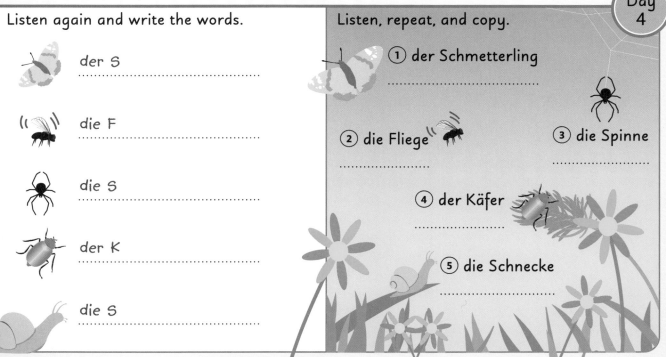

Listen again and write the words.

das S ....

der S ....

der S ....

der S ....

die M ....

Listen, repeat, and copy.

① das Spiel
....

② der Spielstand
....

③ der Schuss
....

④ der Spieler
....

⑤ die Mannschaft
....

Listen again and write the words.

der S ....

die F ....

die S ....

der K ....

die S ....

Listen, repeat, and copy.

① der Schmetterling
....

② die Fliege
....

③ die Spinne
....

④ der Käfer
....

⑤ die Schnecke
....

What can you remember from this week?

---

1. Look at the pictures and circle the correct words.

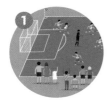

das Spiel
die Mannschaft

der Schuss
der Spielstand

der Schuss
die Mannschaft

der Spieler
der Spielstand

der Spieler
das Spiel

---

2. Look at the pictures and fill in the missing letters.

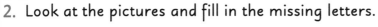

1 d _ r   _ ä e _

2 _ i _   F _ i _ g _

3 d _ r   _ c _ m t e l n _

4 _ i _   S _ h _ e _ k _

5 d _ e _   p _ n _ e _

162

3. Look at the pictures and write the letters in the correct order.

1. m t g i u

   m _ _ _ _ _

2. ü l b e

   ü _ _ _ _

3. w n u d

   w _ _ _ _ _

4. m d e ü

   m _ _ _

5. k a r k n

   k _ _ _ _ _

4. Read the words and mark the correct pictures.

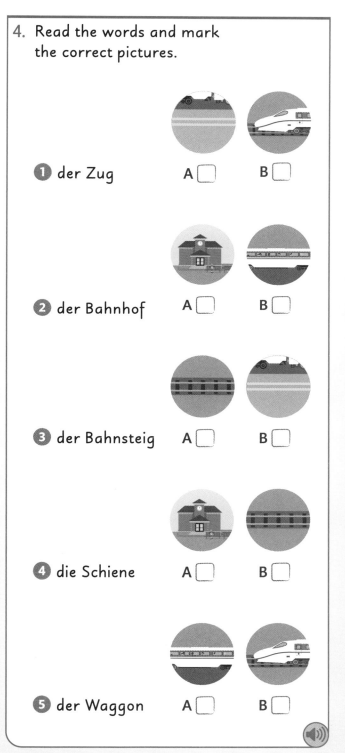

1. der Zug   A ☐   B ☐

2. der Bahnhof   A ☐   B ☐

3. der Bahnsteig   A ☐   B ☐

4. die Schiene   A ☐   B ☐

5. der Waggon   A ☐   B ☐

Day 1

Listen, repeat, and copy.

① die Augenbraue

② der Schnurrbart

③ der Bart

④ der Mund

⑤ das Kinn

Listen again and write the words.

die A ....

der S ....

der B ....

der M ....

das K ....

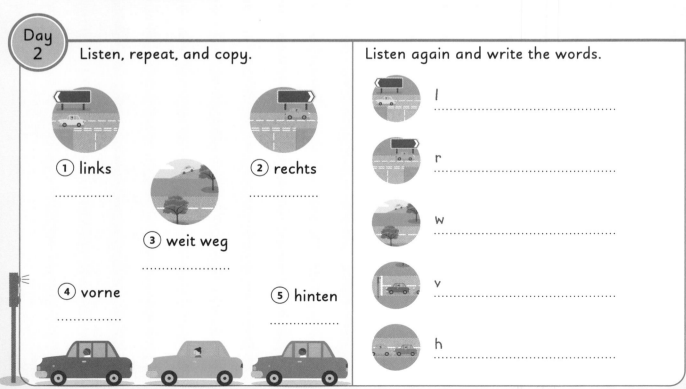

Day 2

Listen, repeat, and copy.

① links

② rechts

③ weit weg

④ vorne

⑤ hinten

Listen again and write the words.

l ....

r ....

w ....

v ....

h ....

Listen again and write the words.

k ....

h ....

v ....

f ....

s ....

Listen, repeat, and copy.

1 kaputt machen
....

2 holen
....

3 verstecken
....

4 füttern
....

5 sich kümmern
....

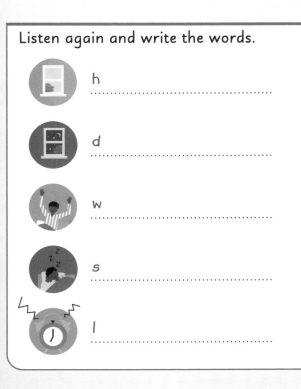

Listen again and write the words.

h ....

d ....

w ....

s ....

l ....

Listen, repeat, and copy.

1 hell
....

2 dunkel
....

3 wach
....

4 schlafend
....

5 laut
....

Day 5

What can you remember from this week?

1. Look at the pictures and write the letters in the correct order.

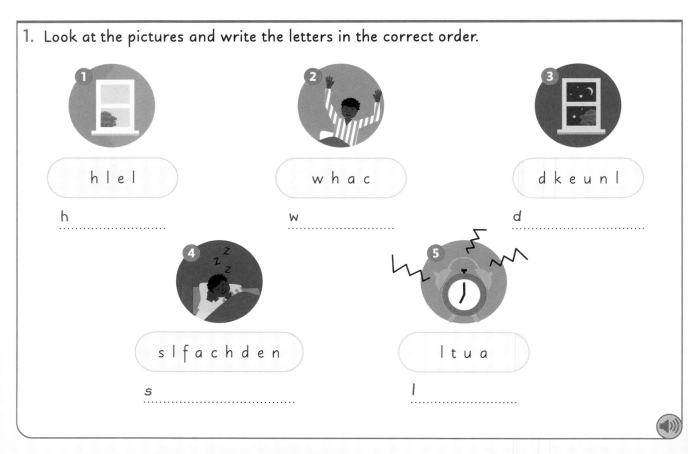

1. h l e l

h ....

2. w h a c

w ....

3. d k e u n l

d ....

4. s l f a c h d e n

s ....

5. l t u a

l ....

2. Match the pictures to the correct words.

holen   verstecken   sich kümmern   füttern   kaputt machen

Week 40

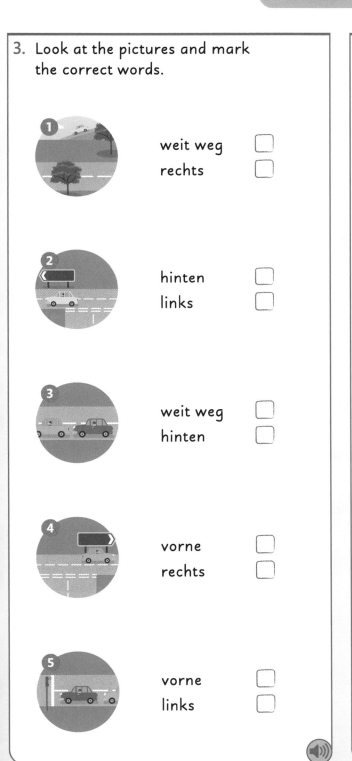

3. Look at the pictures and mark the correct words.

1. weit weg ☐ / rechts ☐
2. hinten ☐ / links ☐
3. weit weg ☐ / hinten ☐
4. vorne ☐ / rechts ☐
5. vorne ☐ / links ☐

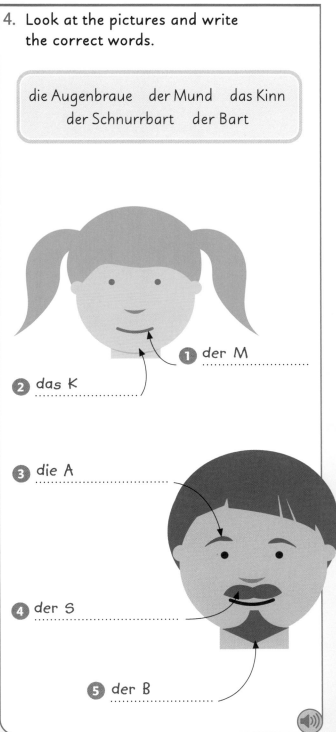

4. Look at the pictures and write the correct words.

die Augenbraue   der Mund   das Kinn
der Schnurrbart   der Bart

1. der M
2. das K
3. die A
4. der S
5. der B

Day 1

Listen, repeat, and copy.

① zuschneiden

....

② wachsen

....

③ gießen

....

④ anpflanzen

⑤ sammeln

....

Listen again and write the words.

z ....

w ....

g ....

a ....

s ....

Day 2

Listen, repeat, and copy.

① die Musik

....

② die Band

....

③ der Musiker

....

④ der Popstar

....

⑤ das Festival

....

Listen again and write the words.

die M ....

die B ....

der M ....

der P ....

das F ....

Week 41

Listen again and write the words.

die H ....

das V ....

g ....

die E ....

die M ....

Listen, repeat, and copy.

① die Hälfte
....

② das Viertel
....

③ ganz
....

④ die Ecke
....

⑤ die Mitte
....

Listen again and write the words.

das H ....

die S ....

die S ....

der P ....

der H ....

Listen, repeat, and copy.

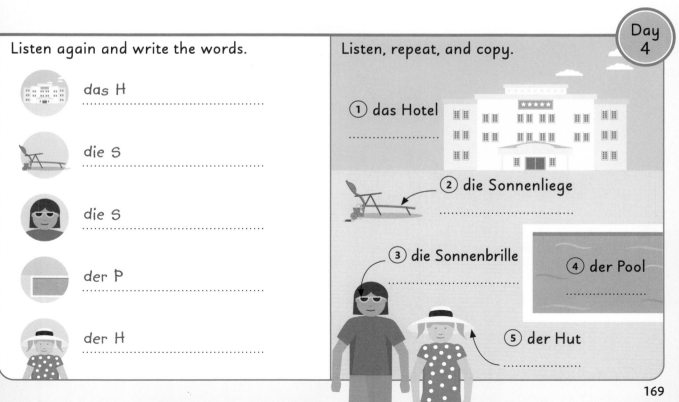

① das Hotel
....

② die Sonnenliege
....

③ die Sonnenbrille
....

④ der Pool
....

⑤ der Hut
....

Day 5

What can you remember from this week?

1. Look at the pictures and write the correct words.

die Mitte   ganz   die Hälfte
die Ecke   das Viertel

1 g ....

2 die E ....

3 die H ....

4 die M ....

5 das V ....

2. Look at the pictures and circle the correct words.

1 die Sonnenbrille
der Pool

2 der Hut
die Sonnenliege

3 das Hotel
der Pool

4 die Sonnenliege
das Hotel

5 der Hut
die Sonnenbrille

3. Read the words and mark the correct pictures.

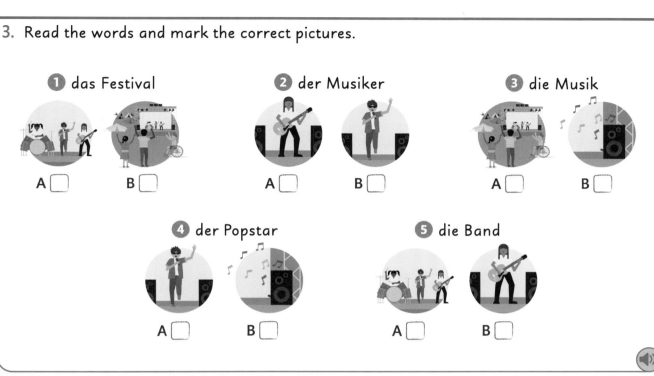

1 das Festival

A ☐ B ☐

2 der Musiker

A ☐ B ☐

3 die Musik

A ☐ B ☐

4 der Popstar

A ☐ B ☐

5 die Band

A ☐ B ☐

4. Look at the pictures and write the correct words.

1 s ....

2 a ....

3 g ....

4 w ....

5 z ....

Day 1

Listen, repeat, and copy.

① der Rauch

....

② der Wohnwagen

....

③ das Zelt

....

④ die Taschenlampe

....

⑤ das Feuer

....

Listen again and write the words.

der R ....

der W ....

das Z ....

die T ....

das F ....

Day 2

Listen, repeat, and copy.

① der Frühling

....

② der Sommer

....

③ der Herbst

....

④ der Winter

....

⑤ die Jahreszeiten

....

Listen again and write the words.

 der F ....

 der S ....

 der H ....

 der W ....

die J ....

Week 42

Listen again and write the words.

`12:01` die U ....

`12:00` die S ....

`12:01` die M ....

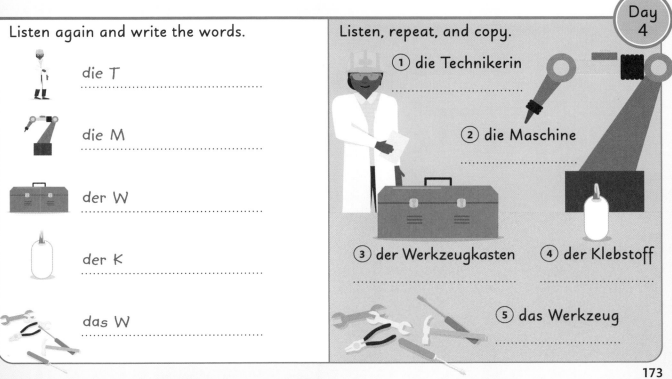 M ....

M ....

Listen, repeat, and copy.

① die Uhr

`12:01`

② die Stunde .... ③ die Minute ....

④ Mittag .... ⑤ Mitternacht ....

Listen again and write the words.

die T ....

die M ....

der W ....

der K ....

das W ....

Listen, repeat, and copy.

① die Technikerin ....

② die Maschine ....

③ der Werkzeugkasten .... ④ der Klebstoff ....

⑤ das Werkzeug ....

Day 5

What can you remember from this week?

1. Look at the pictures and fill in the missing letters.

1 d _ e _ h _

2 _ i t g

3 d _ e _ i u _ e

4 _ i _ t _ r _ a _ h _

5 d _ e _ t _ n _ e

2. Look at the pictures and circle the correct words.

1 das Feuer
das Zelt

2 der Rauch
der Wohnwagen

3 das Zelt
die Taschenlampe

4 der Wohnwagen
die Taschenlampe

5 der Rauch
das Feuer

3. Look at the pictures and write
   the correct words.

1. der S ....

2. der W ....

3. der H ....

4. der F ....

5. die J ....

4. Match the pictures to the correct words.

1.   der Werkzeugkasten

2.   der Klebstoff

3.   die Technikerin

4.   die Maschine

5.   das Werkzeug

Day 1

Listen, repeat, and copy.

① tragen
② wiegen
③ verkaufen

④ kaufen
⑤ geben

Listen again and write the words.

t ....

w ....

v ....

k ....

g ....

Day 2

Listen, repeat, and copy.

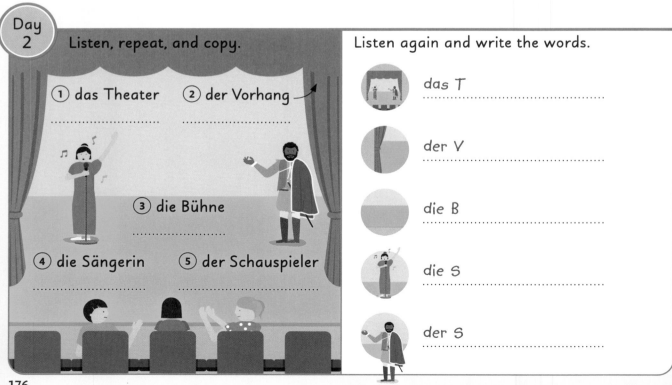

① das Theater
② der Vorhang

③ die Bühne

④ die Sängerin
⑤ der Schauspieler

Listen again and write the words.

das T ....

der V ....

die B ....

die S ....

der S ....

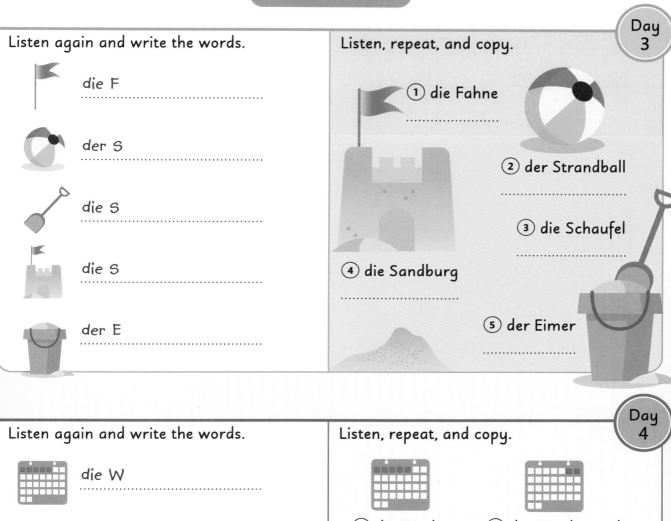

Listen again and write the words.

die F ....

der S ....

die S ....

die S ....

der E ....

Listen, repeat, and copy.

① die Fahne ....

② der Strandball ....

③ die Schaufel ....

④ die Sandburg ....

⑤ der Eimer ....

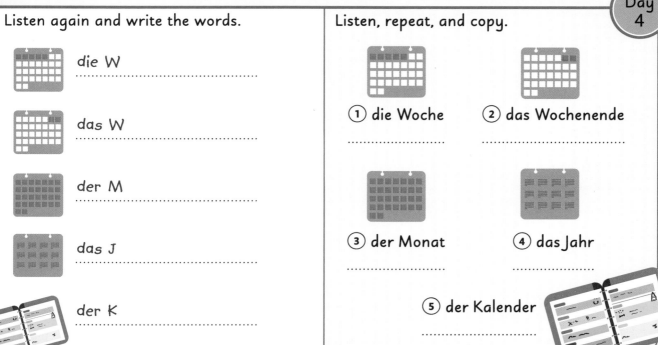

Listen again and write the words.

die W ....

das W ....

der M ....

das J ....

der K ....

Listen, repeat, and copy.

① die Woche ....

② das Wochenende ....

③ der Monat ....

④ das Jahr ....

⑤ der Kalender ....

Day 5

What can you remember from this week?

1. Look at the pictures and write the letters in the correct order.

w g i e e n

w _ _ _ _ _ _

k f e a u n

k _ _ _ _ _ _

g e e n b

g _ _ _ _ _

v k e r e a u n f

v _ _ _ _ _ _ _ _

t g e r a n

t _ _ _ _ _ _

2. Look at the pictures and circle the correct words.

das Theater
der Schauspieler

der Vorhang
die Sängerin

der Schauspieler
die Bühne

die Sängerin
die Bühne

der Vorhang
das Theater

3. Match the pictures to the correct words.

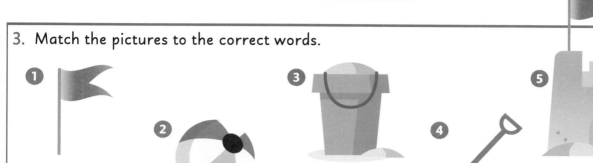

① ② ③ ④ ⑤

der Eimer   die Fahne   die Sandburg   der Strandball   die Schaufel

4. Look at the pictures and write the correct words.

> die Woche   der Monat   das Wochenende   das Jahr   der Kalender

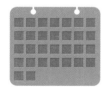 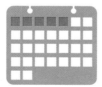 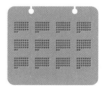

① der M ....   ② die W ....   ③ das J ....

④ der K ....   ⑤ das W ....

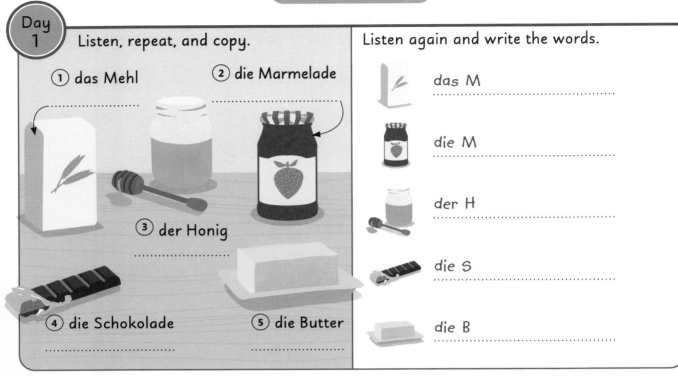

Day 1

Listen, repeat, and copy.

① das Mehl
② die Marmelade
③ der Honig
④ die Schokolade
⑤ die Butter

Listen again and write the words.

das M
die M
der H
die S
die B

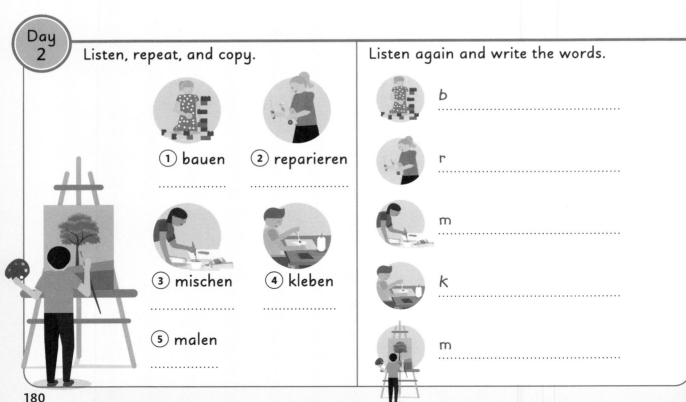

Day 2

Listen, repeat, and copy.

① bauen
② reparieren
③ mischen
④ kleben
⑤ malen

Listen again and write the words.

b
r
m
k
m

Day
3

Listen again and write the words.

 der S ....

 D ....

 M ....

 K ....

 N ....

Listen, repeat, and copy.

 ① der Stundenplan ....

 ② Deutsch ....

③ Mathe ....

 ④ Kunst ....

⑤ Naturwissenschaften ....

Day
4

Listen again and write the words.

 l ....

 s ....

 d ....

 d ....

f ....

Listen, repeat, and copy.

 ① langsam ....

 ② schnell ....

③ dünn ....

④ dick ....

 ⑤ flauschig ....

Day 5 What can you remember from this week?

1. Look at the pictures and circle the correct words.

 ① Deutsch / Kunst

②  Mathe / Naturwissenschaften

③  der Stundenplan / Naturwissenschaften

④ Deutsch / Mathe

⑤ Kunst / der Stundenplan

2. Look at the pictures and fill in the missing letters.

①  b _ u _ n

②  m _ l _ n

③  _ i _ c _ e _

④  r _ p _ r _ e _ e _

⑤  _ _ l _ b _ n

3. Look at the pictures and mark the correct words.

1. die Marmelade ☐
   die Butter ☐
   die Schokolade ☐

2. das Mehl ☐
   der Honig ☐
   die Marmelade ☐

3. die Butter ☐
   die Schokolade ☐
   der Honig ☐

4. das Mehl ☐
   die Butter ☐
   die Marmelade ☐

5. der Honig ☐
   die Schokolade ☐
   das Mehl ☐

4. Look at the pictures and write the correct words.

langsam   flauschig   schnell
         dick   dünn

1. f ....

2. l ....

3. d ....

4. s ....

5. d ....

Day 1

Listen, repeat, and copy.

① die Landkarte

② das Notizbuch

③ das Wörterbuch

④ Schach

⑤ der Student

Listen again and write the words.

die L

das N

das W

S

der S

Day 2

Listen, repeat, and copy.

① der Eingang

② der Ausgang

③ der Parkplatz

④ die Läden

⑤ das Einkaufszentrum

Listen again and write the words.

der E

der A

der P

die L

das E

Listen again and write the words.

 die M ....

 der V ....

 das R ....

 das P ....

die M ....

Listen, repeat, and copy.

 ① die Maske
....

 ② der Verband
....

 ③ das Röntgenbild
....

 ④ das Pflaster
....

⑤ die Medizin
....

Listen again and write the words.

 c ....

 l ....

 s ....

 b ....

 s ....

Listen, repeat, and copy.

① campen
....

② lachen
....

③ sich unterhalten
....

④ brennen
....

⑤ schlafen
....

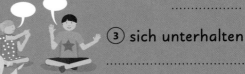
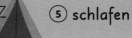

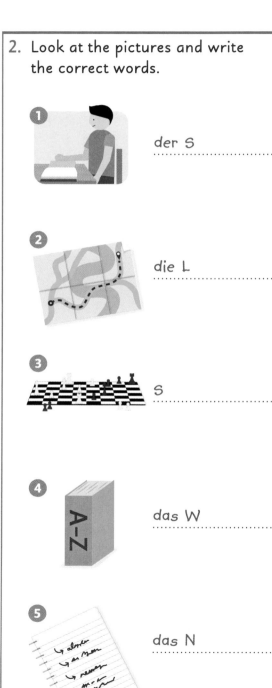

What can you remember from this week?

1. Look at the pictures and circle the correct words.

der Eingang

der Ausgang

der Parkplatz

das Einkaufszentrum

die Läden

der Parkplatz

der Eingang

die Läden

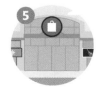

der Ausgang

das Einkaufszentrum

2. Look at the pictures and write the correct words.

1. der S ....

2. die L ....

3. S ....

4. das W ....

5. das N ....

3. Look at the pictures and mark the correct words.

1 
die Medizin ☐
die Maske ☐

2 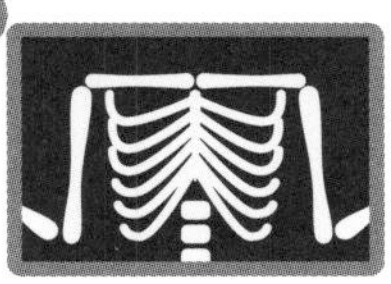
das Pflaster ☐
das Röntgenbild ☐

3 
das Röntgenbild ☐
der Verband ☐

4 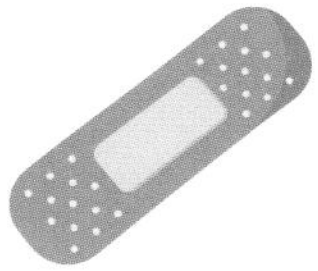
die Medizin ☐
das Pflaster ☐

5 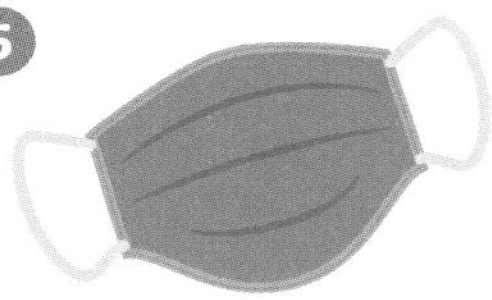
die Maske ☐
der Verband ☐

4. Look at the pictures and fill in the missing letters.

1 _ r _ n _ e _

2 l _ _ c _ e _

3 s _ c _ _ u _ t _ r _ a _ t _ n

4 c _ m _ e _

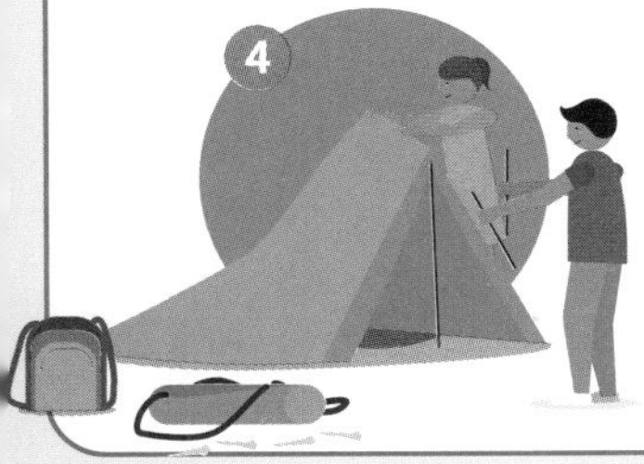

5 s _ _ h _ a _ e _

Day 1

Listen, repeat, and copy.

① die Eule

② das Eichhörnchen

③ der Hirsch

④ der Wolf

⑤ der Fuchs

Listen again and write the words.

die E

das E

der H

der W

der F

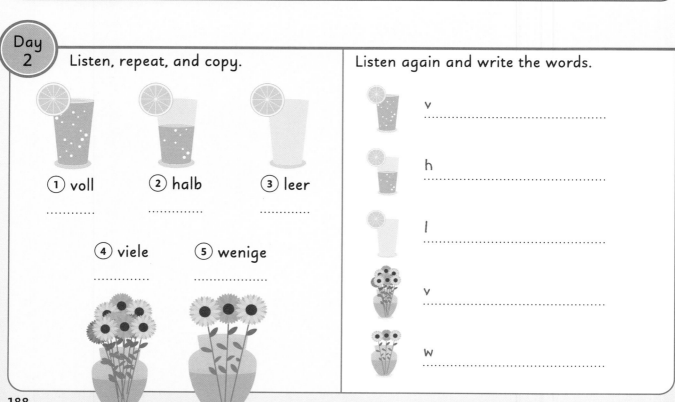

Day 2

Listen, repeat, and copy.

① voll

② halb

③ leer

④ viele

⑤ wenige

Listen again and write the words.

v

h

l

v

w

Listen again and write the words.

die K ....

das S ....

der S ....

die F ....

die M ....

Listen, repeat, and copy.

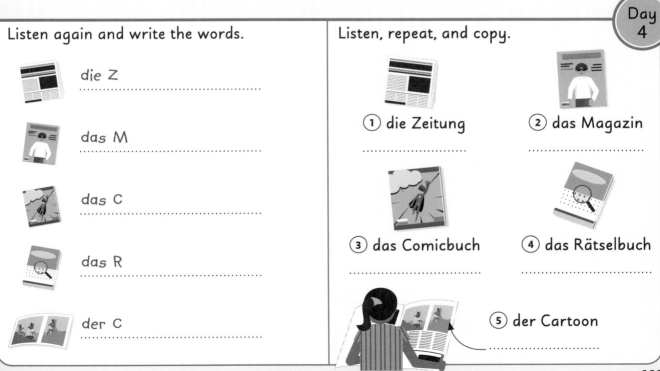

① die Krabbe ....

② das Seegras ....

③ der Seestern ....

④ die Felsen ....

⑤ die Muschel ....

Listen again and write the words.

die Z ....

das M ....

das C ....

das R ....

der C ....

Listen, repeat, and copy.

① die Zeitung ....

② das Magazin ....

③ das Comicbuch ....

④ das Rätselbuch ....

⑤ der Cartoon ....

Day 5

What can you remember from this week?

1. Look at the pictures and write the correct words.

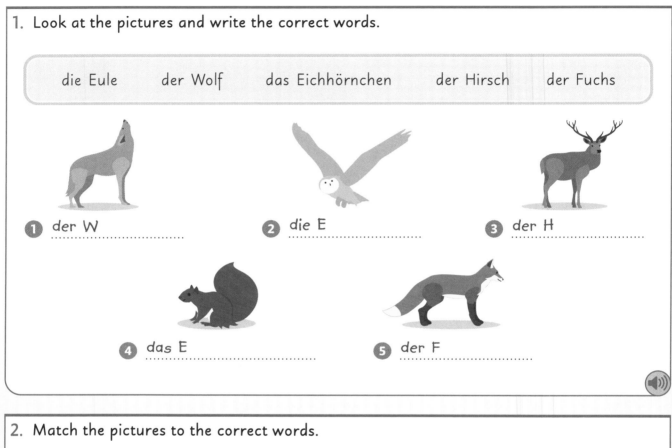

die Eule   der Wolf   das Eichhörnchen   der Hirsch   der Fuchs

1 der W ....

2 die E ....

3 der H ....

4 das E ....

5 der F ....

2. Match the pictures to the correct words.

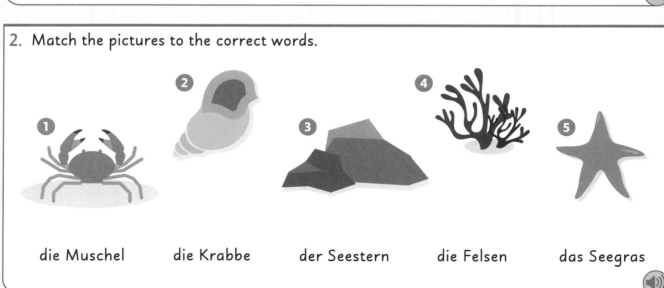

die Muschel   die Krabbe   der Seestern   die Felsen   das Seegras

3. Look at the pictures and write the correct words.

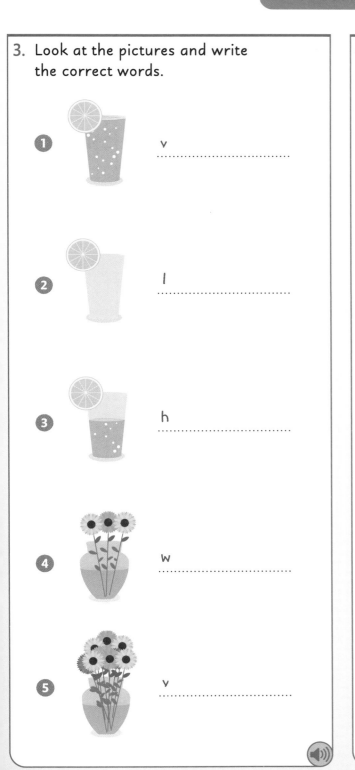

1 v ....

2 l ....

3 h ....

4 w ....

5 v ....

4. Read the words and mark the correct pictures.

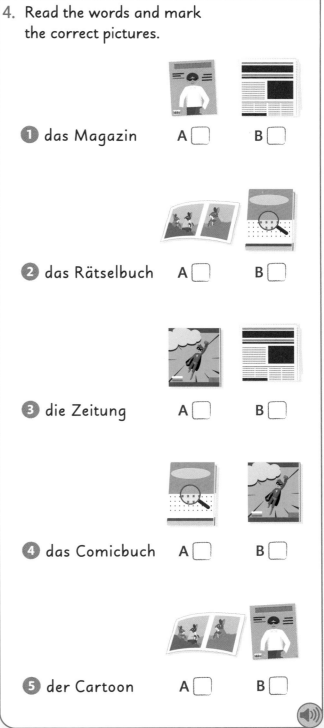

1 das Magazin   A ☐   B ☐

2 das Rätselbuch   A ☐   B ☐

3 die Zeitung   A ☐   B ☐

4 das Comicbuch   A ☐   B ☐

5 der Cartoon   A ☐   B ☐

Week 47

Day 1

Listen, repeat, and copy.

① der Adler
② der Flügel
③ der Schnabel
④ die Klaue
⑤ das Nest

Listen again and write the words.

der A

der F

der S

die K

das N

Day 2

Listen, repeat, and copy.

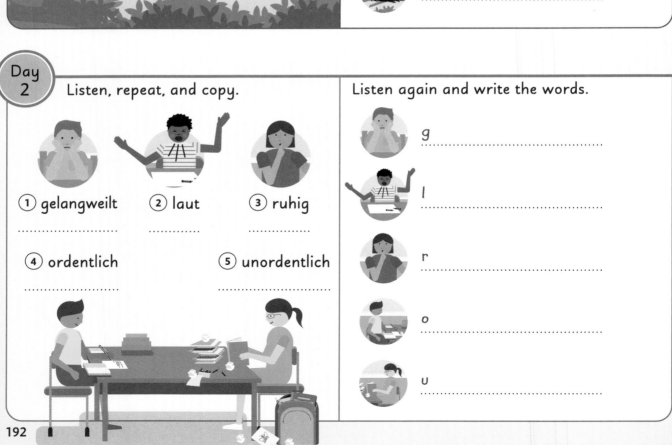

① gelangweilt
② laut
③ ruhig
④ ordentlich
⑤ unordentlich

Listen again and write the words.

g

l

r

o

u

Week 47

Day 3

Listen again and write the words.

 das S ....

 das S ....

 E ....

 das S ....

 das S ....

Listen, repeat, and copy.

① das Skifahren   ② das Schlittenfahren
....

③ Eishockey   ④ das Schlittschuhlaufen
....

 ⑤ das Snowboardfahren
....

Day 4

Listen again and write the words.

 G ....

 E ....

 W ....

 F ....

 die F ....

Listen, repeat, and copy.

① Geschichte
....

② Erdkunde
....

③ Werken
....

④ Fremdsprachen
....

 ⑤ die Fächer
....

193

Week 47

Day 5 What can you remember from this week?

1. Look at the pictures and mark the correct words.

 **①**
Erdkunde ☐
die Fächer ☐

 ②
Fremdsprachen ☐
Werken ☐

③
Geschichte ☐
Erdkunde ☐

 ④
Fremdsprachen ☐
Geschichte ☐

 **⑤**
Werken ☐
die Fächer ☐

2. Look at the pictures and fill in the missing letters.

 ①
d _ s _ e _ t

 ②
_ e _ S _ h _ a _ e

 ③
d _ r _ _ _ g _ _
(with r, g given)

 ④
_ i _ K _ a _ e

 **⑤**
d _ r _ d _ e _

194

3. Look at the pictures and write the correct words.

① l ....

② r ....

③ u ....

④ o ....

⑤ g ....

4. Read the words and mark the correct pictures.

① das Schlittenfahren

A ☐   B ☐

② das Snowboardfahren

A ☐   B ☐

③ das Skifahren

A ☐   B ☐

④ das Schlittschuhlaufen

A ☐   B ☐

⑤ Eishockey

A ☐   B ☐

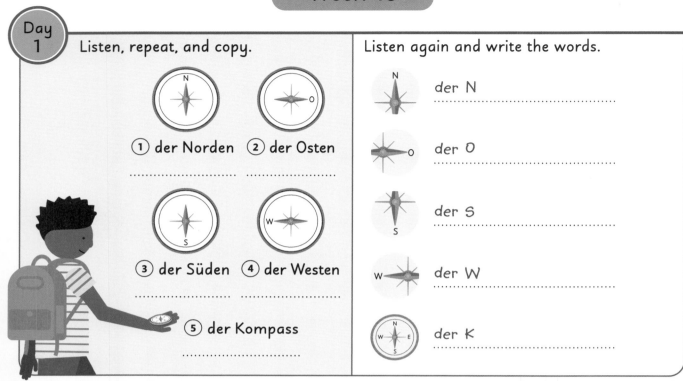

Day 1

Listen, repeat, and copy.

① der Norden ② der Osten

③ der Süden ④ der Westen

⑤ der Kompass

Listen again and write the words.

der N

der O

der S

der W

der K

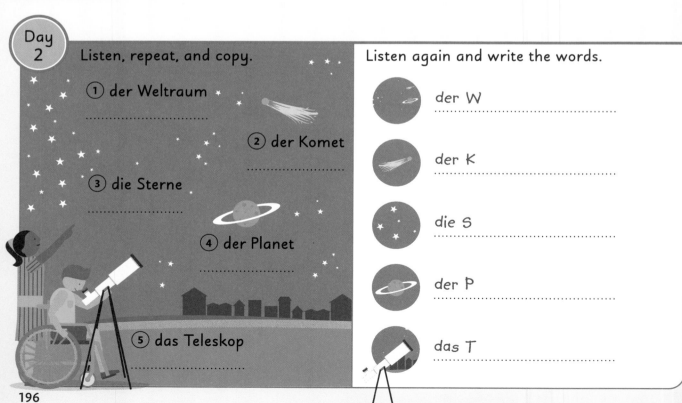

Day 2

Listen, repeat, and copy.

① der Weltraum

② der Komet

③ die Sterne

④ der Planet

⑤ das Teleskop

Listen again and write the words.

der W

der K

die S

der P

das T

Listen again and write the words.

 die H ....

 die H ....

 der R ....

 das A ....

 die A ....

Listen, repeat, and copy.

① die Halskette ....

② die Handtasche ....

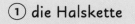

③ der Ring ....

④ das Armband ....

⑤ die Armbanduhr ....

Listen again and write the words.

 der J ....

 die D ....

 die K ....

 die F ....

 die B ....

Listen, repeat, and copy.

① der Journalist ....

② die Designerin ....

③ die Künstlerin ....

④ die Fotografin ....

⑤ die Berufe ....

Day 5 What can you remember from this week?

1. Look at the picture and write the correct words.

der Westen

der Norden

der Kompass

der Süden

der Osten

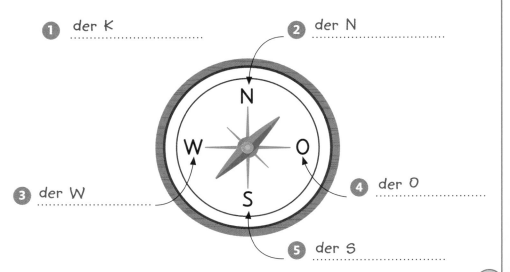

① der K ....

② der N ....

③ der W ....

④ der O ....

⑤ der S ....

2. Look at the pictures and circle the correct words.

① die Berufe
die Künstlerin

② die Fotografin
die Designerin

③ der Journalist
die Designerin

④ die Künstlerin
der Journalist

⑤ die Berufe
die Fotografin

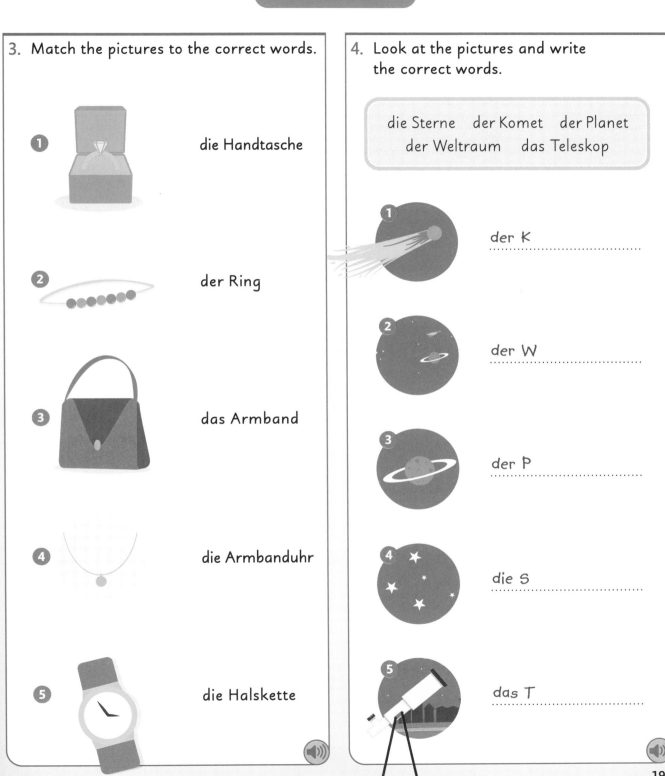

3. Match the pictures to the correct words.

1 die Handtasche

2 der Ring

3 das Armband

4 die Armbanduhr

5 die Halskette

4. Look at the pictures and write the correct words.

die Sterne   der Komet   der Planet
der Weltraum   das Teleskop

1 der K ....

2 der W ....

3 der P ....

4 die S ....

5 das T ....

Day 1

Listen, repeat, and copy.

1. die Schnurrhaare
2. das Halsband
3. das Fell
4. die Pfote
5. der Schwanz

Listen again and write the words.

die S

das H

das F

die P

der S

Day 2

Listen, repeat, and copy.

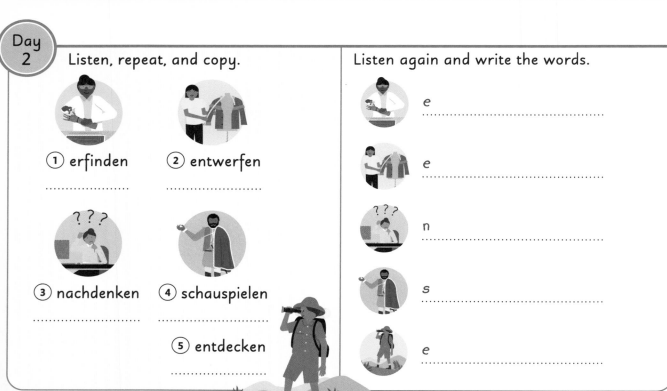

1. erfinden
2. entwerfen
3. nachdenken
4. schauspielen
5. entdecken

Listen again and write the words.

e

e

n

s

e

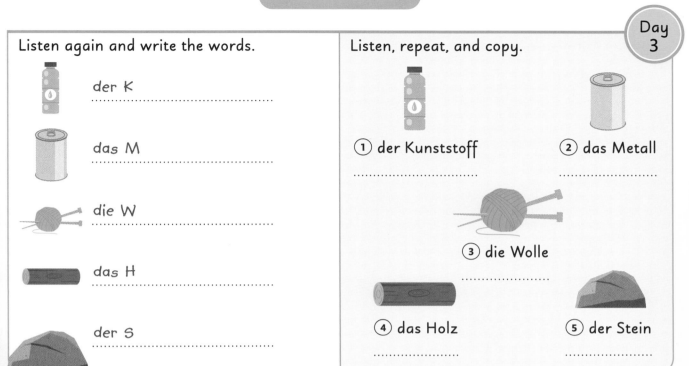

Day 3

Listen again and write the words.

der K ....

das M ....

die W ....

das H ....

der S ....

Listen, repeat, and copy.

① der Kunststoff
....

② das Metall
....

③ die Wolle
....

④ das Holz
....

⑤ der Stein
....

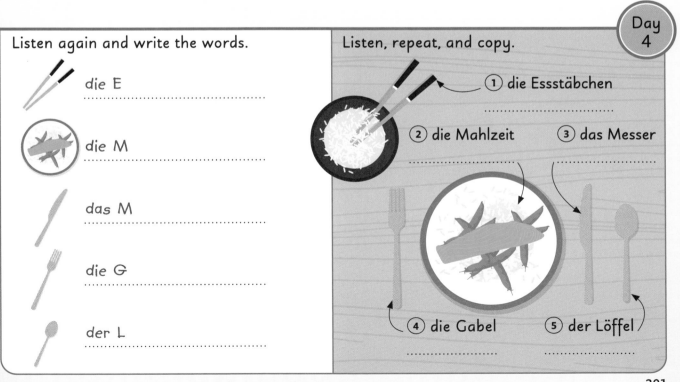

Day 4

Listen again and write the words.

die E ....

die M ....

das M ....

die G ....

der L ....

Listen, repeat, and copy.

① die Essstäbchen
....

② die Mahlzeit
....

③ das Messer

④ die Gabel
....

⑤ der Löffel
....

Day 5

What can you remember from this week?

1. Read the words and mark the correct pictures.

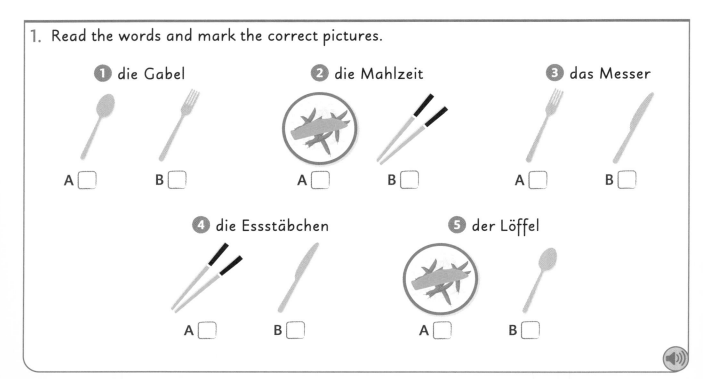

1 die Gabel
A ☐   B ☐

2 die Mahlzeit
A ☐   B ☐

3 das Messer
A ☐   B ☐

4 die Essstäbchen
A ☐   B ☐

5 der Löffel
A ☐   B ☐

2. Look at the pictures and fill in the missing letters.

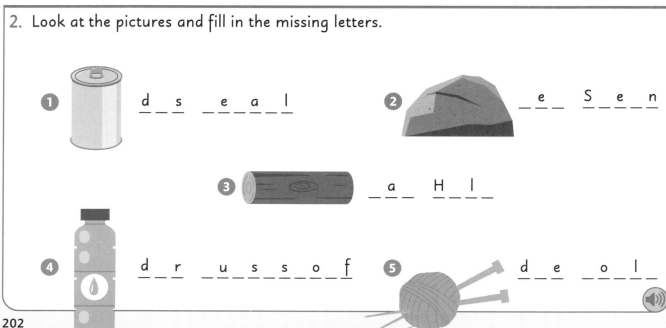

1 d _ s _ e _ a _ l

2 _ e _ S _ e _ n

3 _ a _ H _ l _

4 d _ r _ u _ s _ s _ o _ f

5 d _ e _ _ o _ l _

3. Look at the pictures and mark the correct words.

1. das Halsband ☐
   die Schnurrhaare ☐
   das Fell ☐

2. das Halsband ☐
   der Schwanz ☐
   die Pfote ☐

3. der Schwanz ☐
   das Fell ☐
   die Schnurrhaare ☐

4. die Schnurrhaare ☐
   das Halsband ☐
   die Pfote ☐

5. das Fell ☐
   die Pfote ☐
   der Schwanz ☐

4. Look at the pictures and write the letters in the correct order.

1. e e n r d f i n

   e ....

2. n d h e e a n k c n

   n ....

3. e t n d e n c k e

   e ....

4. s c h s p a n u i e l e

   s ....

5. e f e n n t e r w

   e ....

Week 50

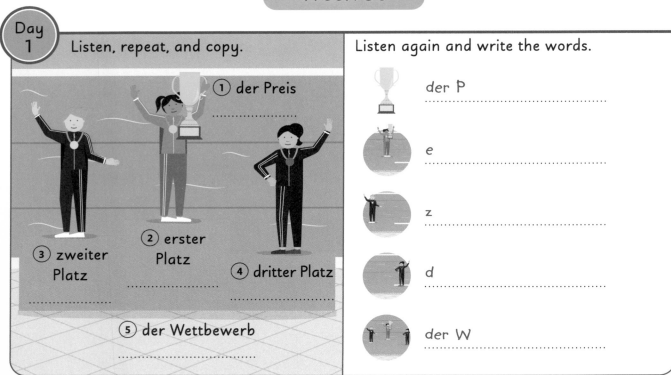

Day 1

Listen, repeat, and copy.

① der Preis

③ zweiter Platz

② erster Platz

④ dritter Platz

⑤ der Wettbewerb

Listen again and write the words.

der P

e

z

d

der W

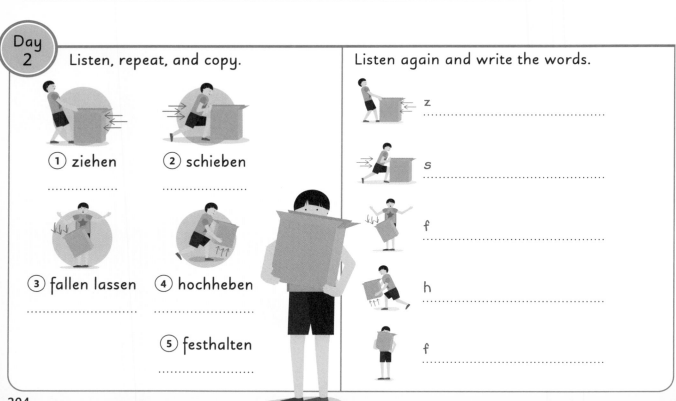

Day 2

Listen, repeat, and copy.

① ziehen

② schieben

③ fallen lassen

④ hochheben

⑤ festhalten

Listen again and write the words.

z

s

f

h

f

Week 50

Listen again and write the words.

der K ....

der F ....

die R ....

der P ....

die R ....

Listen, repeat, and copy.

① der Klempner
....

② der Frisör
....

③ die Rezeptionistin
....

④ der Postbote
....

⑤ die Reinigungskraft
....

Listen again and write the words.

S ....

das M ....

P ....

b ....

t ....

Listen, repeat, and copy.

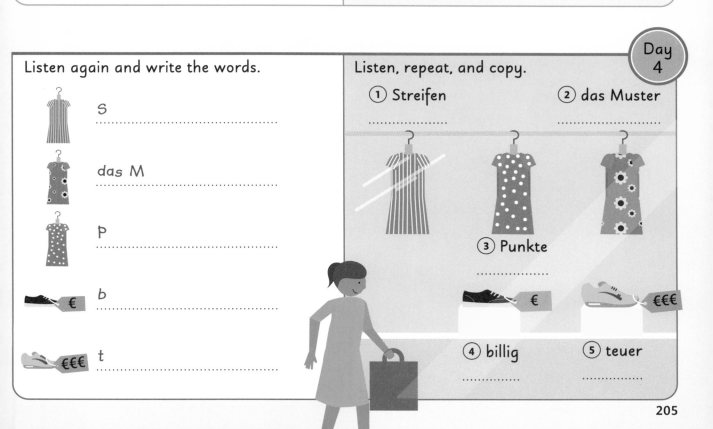

① Streifen
....

② das Muster
....

③ Punkte
....

④ billig
....

⑤ teuer
....

Day 5

What can you remember from this week?

1. Look at the pictures and circle the correct words.

1. schieben / ziehen

2. festhalten / fallen lassen

3. hochheben / schieben

4. fallen lassen / ziehen

5. festhalten / hochheben

2. Look at the pictures and write the correct words.

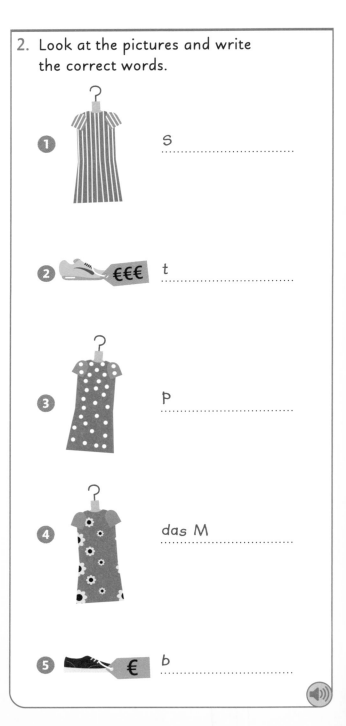

1. s ....

2. t ....

3. p ....

4. das M ....

5. b ....

3. Look at the pictures and write the correct words.

der Preis   erster Platz   der Wettbewerb   zweiter Platz   dritter Platz

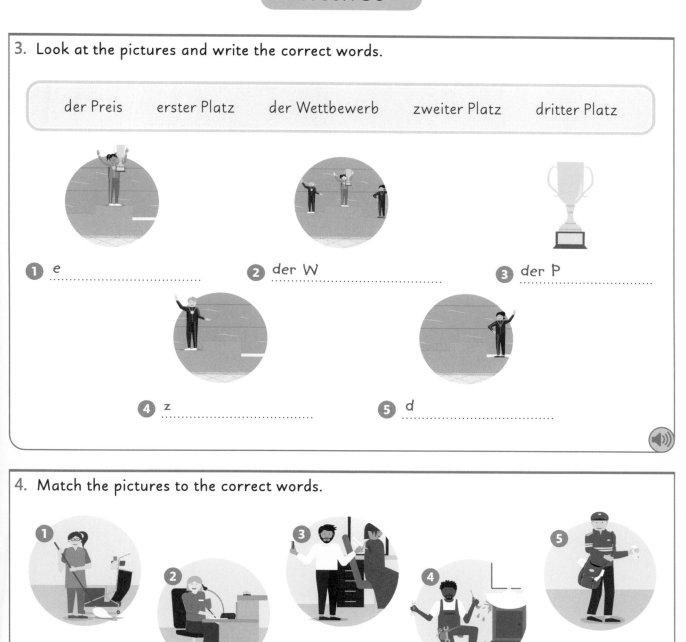

1 e _____

2 der W _____

3 der P _____

4 z _____

5 d _____

4. Match the pictures to the correct words.

der Frisör

der Postbote

die Reinigungskraft

die Rezeptionistin

der Klempner

Day 1

Listen, repeat, and copy.

① die Königin ② der König

③ die Prinzessin ④ der Prinz

⑤ die Krone

Listen again and write the words.

die K

der K

die P

der P

die K

Day 2

Listen, repeat, and copy.

① weich ② hart

③ stark ④ schwach

⑤ kaputt

Listen again and write the words.

w

h

s

s

k

Day 3

Listen again and write the words.

s ....

r ....

e ....

a ....

w ....

Listen, repeat, and copy.

① suchen
....

② reparieren
....

③ einschalten
....

④ ausschalten
....

⑤ wechseln
....

Day 4

Listen again and write the words.

die K ....

der R ....

der K ....

die T ....

der G ....

Listen, repeat, and copy.

① die Krawatte
....

② der Reißverschluss
....

③ der Knopf
....

④ die Tasche
....

⑤ der Gürtel
....

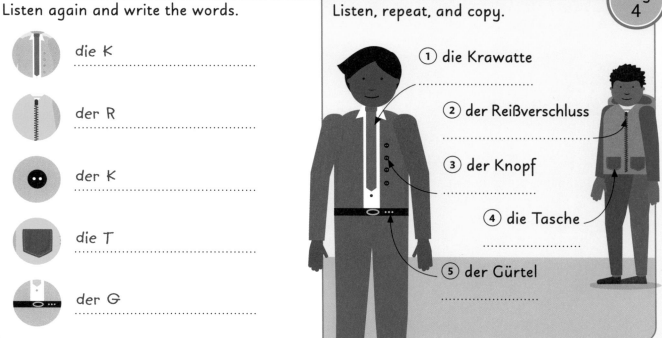

Day 5 What can you remember from this week?

---

1. Look at the pictures and fill in the missing letters.

   w _ c _ s _ l _

   _ u _ h _ n

   e _ n _ c _ a _ t _ n

   _ u _ s _ h _ l _ e _

   r _ p _ r _ e _ e _

---

2. Look at the pictures and circle the correct words.

   die Krawatte
der Knopf

   die Tasche
der Knopf

   der Gürtel
der Reißverschluss

   die Tasche
der Reißverschluss

   die Krawatte
der Gürtel

3. Look at the pictures and write the letters in the correct order.

1. s r k t a

   s _ _ _ _ _

2. w h e c i

   w _ _ _ _ _

3. h t a r

   h _ _ _ _

4. k t a u t p

   k _ _ _ _ _

5. s w c h a c h

   s _ _ _ _ _ _ _

4. Look at the pictures and mark the correct words.

1. die Prinzessin ☐
   die Krone ☐

2. die Königin ☐
   der König ☐

3. die Prinzessin ☐
   der Prinz ☐

4. die Krone ☐
   der König ☐

5. die Königin ☐
   der Prinz ☐

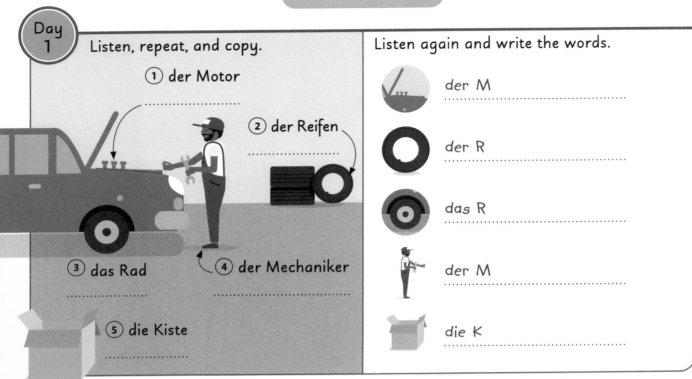

Day 1

Listen, repeat, and copy.

① der Motor

② der Reifen

③ das Rad

④ der Mechaniker

⑤ die Kiste

Listen again and write the words.

der M

der R

das R

der M

die K

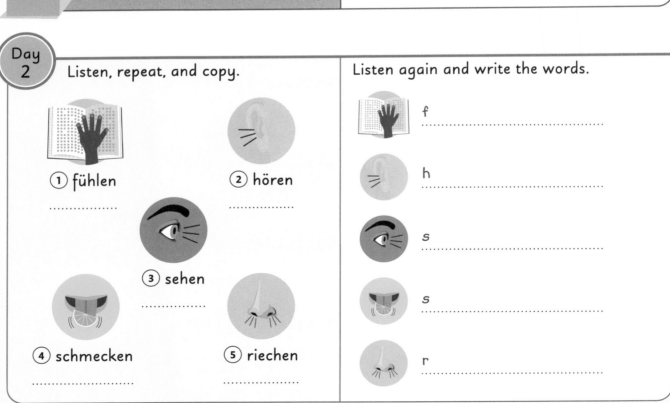

Day 2

Listen, repeat, and copy.

① fühlen

② hören

③ sehen

④ schmecken

⑤ riechen

Listen again and write the words.

f

h

s

s

r

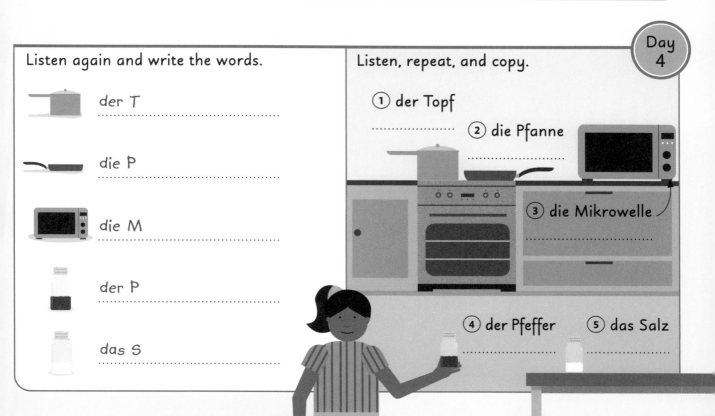

Day 3

Listen again and write the words.

die G ....

die T ....

die I ....

das K ....

die M ....

Listen, repeat, and copy.

① die Geige

② die Trommel

③ die Instrumente

④ das Konzert

⑤ die Musik

Day 4

Listen again and write the words.

der T ....

die P ....

die M ....

der P ....

das S ....

Listen, repeat, and copy.

① der Topf

② die Pfanne

③ die Mikrowelle

④ der Pfeffer

⑤ das Salz

Day 5

What can you remember from this week?

1. Look at the pictures and write the correct words.

1. der P ....

2. das S ....

3. die M ....

4. der T ....

5. die P ....

2. Match the pictures to the correct words.

1. die Musik

2. die Trommel

3. die Geige

4. das Konzert

5. die Instrumente

3. Look at the pictures and write the correct words.

| fühlen | schmecken | hören | riechen | sehen |

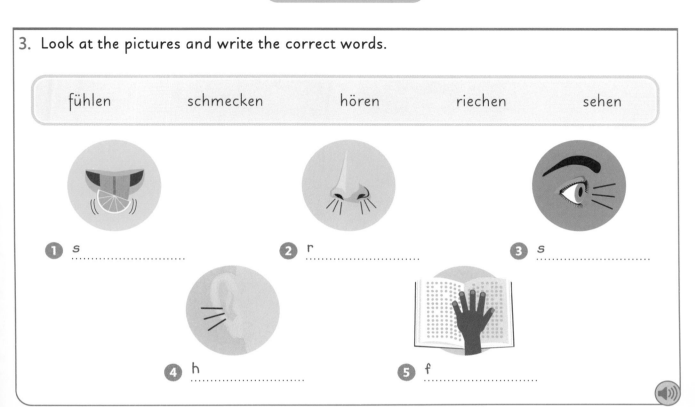

1 s ....

2 r ....

3 s ....

4 h ....

5 f ....

4. Read the words and mark the correct pictures.

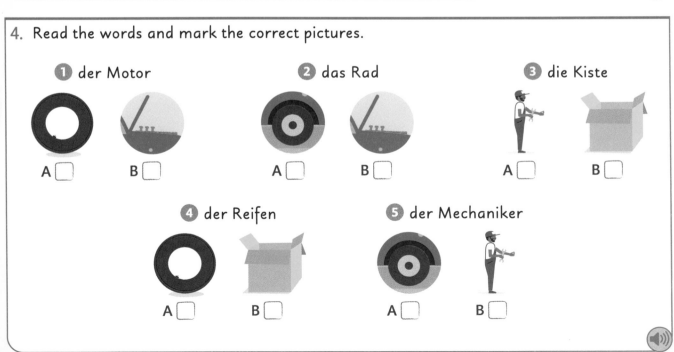

1 der Motor   A ☐   B ☐

2 das Rad   A ☐   B ☐

3 die Kiste   A ☐   B ☐

4 der Reifen   A ☐   B ☐

5 der Mechaniker   A ☐   B ☐

Numbers

Listen, repeat, and copy.

0 ① null

10 ② zehn

20 ③ zwanzig

30 ④ dreißig

40 ⑤ vierzig

50 ⑥ fünfzig

60 ⑦ sechzig

70 ⑧ siebzig

80 ⑨ achtzig

90 ⑩ neunzig

91 ⑪ einundneunzig

92 ⑫ zweiundneunzig

93 ⑬ dreiundneunzig

94 ⑭ vierundneunzig

95 ⑮ fünfundneunzig

96 ⑯ sechsundneunzig

97 ⑰ siebenundneunzig

98 ⑱ achtundneunzig

99 ⑲ neunundneunzig

100 ⑳ hundert

1000 ㉑ tausend

1000000 ㉒ eine Million

Days

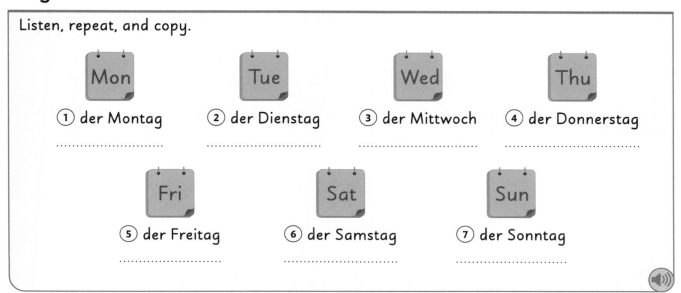

Listen, repeat, and copy.

① der Montag

② der Dienstag

③ der Mittwoch

④ der Donnerstag

⑤ der Freitag

⑥ der Samstag

⑦ der Sonntag

Months

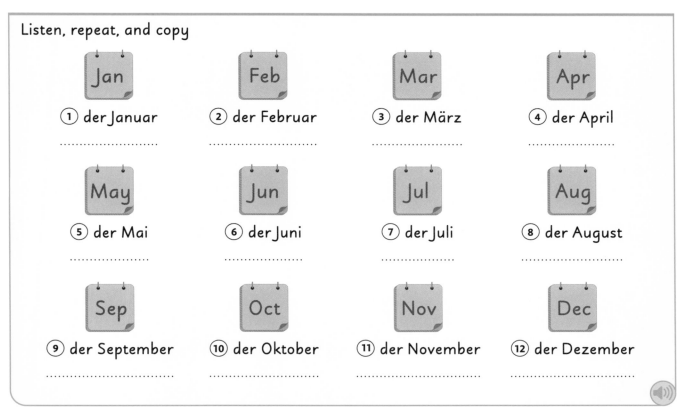

Listen, repeat, and copy

① der Januar

② der Februar

③ der März

④ der April

⑤ der Mai

⑥ der Juni

⑦ der Juli

⑧ der August

⑨ der September

⑩ der Oktober

⑪ der November

⑫ der Dezember

English word list

KEY

adj	adjective
n	noun
num	number
prep	preposition
v	verb

A

act *v* 49
action figure *n* 2
actor *n* 43
add *v* 10
address *n* 30
afraid *adj* 12
afternoon *n* 8
airplane *n* 38
airport *n* 38
alphabet *n* 2
ambulance *n* 25
angry *adj* 12
animals *n* 10
answer *v* 5
ant *n* 17
apartment *n* 12
apartment building *n* 12
apple *n* 1
apps *n* 21
April *n* **p217**
arm *n* 6
armchair *n* 7
arrive *v* 38
art *n* 44
artist *n* 48
ask *v* 17
asleep *adj* 40

astronaut *n* 34
August *n* **p217**
aunt *n* 14
awake *adj* 40

B

baby *n* 7
back *adj* 40
back *n* 23
backpack *n* 5
badminton *n* 6
balcony *n* 12
ball *n* 6
balloon *n* 16
banana *n* 1
band *n* 41
bandage *n* 45
band-aid *n* 45
bank *n* 35
barn *n* 10
baseball *n* 6
baseball cap *n* 11
basement *n* 22
basket *n* 33
basketball *n* 6
bat *n* 15
bathroom *n* 4
bathtub *n* 26
beach *n* 15
beach ball *n* 43
beak *n* 47
beans *n* 29
bear *n* 8
beard *n* 40
beautiful *adj* 11
bed *n* 8
bedroom *n* 4
bee *n* 17
beetle *n* 39
behind *prep* 12
belt *n* 51
bench *n* 21
between *prep* 28

bicycle *n* 21
big *adj* 11
bird *n* 19
birthday party *n* 19
black *adj* 38
black *n* 4
blanket *n* 34
blonde *adj* 38
blue *n* 1
board *n* 1
board game *n* 2
boat *n* 27
body *n* 6
book *n* 5
bookcase *n* 7
bookstore *n* 21
boots *n* 26
bored *adj* 47
borrow *v* 35
bottle *n* 33
bottom *adj* 35
bounce *v* 9
bowl *n* 33
box *n* 52
boy *n* 7
bracelet *n* 48
branch *n* 13
brave *adj* 39
bread *n* 14
break *v* 40
breakfast *n* 12
bridge *n* 34
bring *v* 38
broken *adj* 51
bronze *n* 36
brother *n* 14
brown *adj* 38
brown *n* 4
brush *n* 37
brush my teeth *v* 25
bucket *n* 43
build *v* 44
burger *n* 7
burn *v* 45
bus *n* 24
bus station *n* 24
bus stop *n* 32
butter *n* 44
butterfly *n* 39

button *n* 51
buy *v* 43

C

cabbage *n* 23
cabinet *n* 31
café *n* 21
cake *n* 19
calendar *n* 8
camel *n* 24
camera *n* 34
camp *v* 45
candle *n* 19
candy *n* 16
car *n* 25
card *n* 19
carnival *n* 28
carpet *n* 19
carrot *n* 15
carry *v* 43
cart *n* 33
cartoon *n* 46
castle *n* 27
cat *n* 6, 16
catch *v* 9
catch a bus *v* 13
caterpillar *n* 17
cave *n* 23
ceiling *n* 30
cell phone *n* 31
center *n* 41
cereal *n* 12
chair *n* 16, 19
change *v* 51
charger *n* 31
chat *v* 45
cheap *adj* 50
check *v* 10
cheese *n* 38
chef *n* 32
cherry *n* 20
chess *n* 45
chest *n* 20
chicken *n* 4
chicken *n* 7
child *n* 18
children *n* 10
chin *n* 40

chocolate n 44
choose v 17
chopsticks n 49
circle n 17
circle v 10
circus n 28
city n 33
clap v 19
class n 1
classmate n 2
classroom n 2
claw n 47
clean adj 11
clean v 22
cleaner n 50
climb v 15
clock n 16, 42
close v 8
clothes n 7
cloud n 31
cloudy adj 28
clown n 28
coat n 26
coconut n 5
coffee n 36
cold adj 35
cold n 30
collar n 49
collect v 41
college n 33
color v 3
colors n 1
comb n 37
comet n 48
comic book n 46
compass n 48
competition n 50
complete v 29
computer n 28
concert n 52
cook v 16
cookie n 36
corner n 41
correct adj 22
couch n 7
cough n 30
count v 3
countryside n 30
cousin n 14

cow n 4
crab n 46
crayon n 2
crocodile n 24
cross v 10
crosswalk n 32
crown n 51
cry v 26
cup n 33
curly adj 18
curtains n 43
cushion n 19
cut v 41
cycle v 13

D

dad n 3
dance v 11
dancing n 14
dark adj 40
date n 22
daughter n 3
day n 8
December n p217
deer n 46
dentist n 29
desert n 24
design n 47
design v 49
designer n 48
desk n 16
diary n 43
dictionary n 45
different adj 25
dining room n 4
dinner n 14
dinosaur n 10
dirty adj 11
do homework v 22
doctor n 18
dog n 6, 16
doll n 2
dolphin n 20
don't like v 37
donkey n 19
door n 30
downstairs n 22
dragonfly n 17

draw v 3
drawing n 14
dream v 25
dress n 9
drink v 16
drinks n 17
drive v 13
driver n 24
drop v 50
drum n 52
dry adj 35
dry v 16
duck n 37
DVD n 24

E

eagle n 47
ear n 11
earache n 30
Earth n 34
east n 48
eat v 16
e-book n 21
egg n 12
eggplant n 23
eight num 2
eighteen num 4
eighty num p216
elbow n 20
elephant n 5
elevator n 12
eleven num 3
email n 21
email v 24
empty adj 46
engine n 52
engineer n 42
English n 44
entrance n 45
envelope n 30
eraser n 5
evening n 8
excited adj 27
exit n 45
expensive adj 50
explore v 49
eye n 11
eyebrow n 40

F

face n 11
factory n 35
fall n 42
fall over v 26
family n 3
far adj 40
farm n 10
farmer n 19
fast adj 44
fat adj 44
father n 3
faucet n 27
favorite adj 25
February n p217
feed v 40
feel v 52
fence n 14
festival n 41
fetch v 40
few adj 46
field n 10
field hockey n 6
fifteen num 3
fifty num p216
find v 29
fingers n 20
finish v 33
fire n 42
fire engine n 25
fire station n 35
firefighter n 18
first adj 50
fish n 29
fish v 18
fishing n 29
fishing rod n 29
five num 1
fix v 44
flag n 43
flashlight n 42
floor n 30
flour n 44
flower n 13
fly n 39
fly v 18
fog n 13
foggy adj 28
food n 32

foot *n* 23
forest *n* 27
fork *n* 49
forty *num* **p216**
four *num* 1
fourteen *num* 3
fox *n* 46
Friday **p217**
friendly *adj* 27
friends *n* 18
fries *n* 7
frog *n* 8, 37
front *adj* 40
fruit *n* 13
full *adj* 46
fur *n* 49
furry *adj* 44

G

game *n* 16
garlic *n* 23
gate *n* 25
geography *n* 47
get dressed *v* 25
get off *v* 36
get on *v* 36
giraffe *n* 5
girl *n* 7
give *v* 38, 43
glass *n* 33
glasses *n* 37
gloves *n* 26
glue *n* 42
glue *v* 44
goat *n* 4
goggles *n* 22
gold *n* 36
goldfish *n* 6
golf *n* 23
gorilla *n* 26
granddaughter *n* 9
grandfather *n* 9
grandmother *n* 9
grandparents *n* 9
grandson *n* 9
grapes *n* 1
grass *n* 37
gray *adj* 38

green *n* 1
greet *v* 38
ground *n* 31
ground floor *n* 12
group *n* 18
grow *v* 41
grown-up *n* 18
gym *n* 31
gymnastics *n* 23

H

hair *n* 18
hairdresser *n* 50
half *adj* 46
half *n* 41
hall *n* 22
hand *n* 20
happy *adj* 12
hard *adj* 51
hat *n* 41
head *n* 6
headache *n* 30
headphones *n* 31
hear *v* 52
helmet *n* 15
help *v* 26
hide *v* 40
hills *n* 30
hippo *n* 5
history *n* 47
hit *v* 9
hobbies *n* 14
hockey stick *n* 36
hold *v* 50
home *n* 14
honey *n* 44
hop *v* 32
horse *n* 4
hospital *n* 35
hot *adj* 35
hotel *n* 41
hour *n* 42
house *n* 3
hungry *adj* 27
hurry *v* 36
hurt *v* 26

I

ice *n* 32
ice cream *n* 28
ice hockey *n* 47
ice skates *n* 36
ice-skating *n* 47
ill *adj* 39
in *prep* 12
in front of *prep* 12
insects *n* 31
inside *prep* 28
instruments *n* 52
invent *v* 49
invitation *n* 16
island *n* 15

J

jacket *n* 11
jam *n* 44
January *n* **p217**
jeans *n* 7
jellyfish *n* 20
jewelry *n* 37
jobs *n* 48
join *v* 29
journalist *n* 48
juice *n* 17
July *n* **p217**
jump *v* 15
June *n* **p217**
jungle *n* 8

K

kangaroo *n* 26
key *n* 30
keyboard *n* 28
kick *n* 39
kick *v* 9
king *n* 51
kitchen *n* 4
kite *n* 6
kitten *n* 16
kiwi *n* 5
knee *n* 23
knife *n* 49

L

ladder *n* 25
ladybug *n* 17
lake *n* 27
lamp *n* 16
land *v* 36
languages *n* 47
laptop *n* 31
laugh *v* 45
leaf *n* 13
learn *v* 5
left *adj* 40
leg *n* 6
lemon *n* 20
lemonade *n* 17
lesson *n* 27
letter *n* 30
letters *n* 2
lettuce *n* 38
library *n* 31
life jacket *n* 29
lift *v* 50
light *adj* 40
lights *n* 19
like *v* 37
lime *n* 20
lion *n* 5
lips *n* 11
listen *v* 5
little *adj* 35
living room *n* 4
lizard *n* 23
long *adj* 18
look after *v* 40
look for *v* 51
loud *adj* 40
lounge chair *n* 41
lunch *n* 13

M

machine *n* 42
magazine *n* 46
mail carrier *n* 50
make the bed *v* 25
man *n* 7
mango *n* 5
many *adj* 46

map *n* 45
March *n* **p217**
market *n* 30
mask *n* 45
mat *n* 25
match *n* 39
match *v* 10
math *n* 44
May *n* **p217**
meal *n* 49
meat *n* 29
meatballs *n* 14
mechanic *n* 52
medicine *n* 45
meet *v* 34
men *n* 10
menu *n* 32
message *n* 21
metal *n* 49
microwave *n* 52
midday *n* 42
middle *adj* 35
midnight *n* 42
milk *n* 36
milkshake *n* 17
minute *n* 42
mirror *n* 26
mistake *n* 22
mix *v* 44
mom *n* 3
Monday *n* **p217**
money *n* 33
monkey *n* 8
monster *n* 10
month *n* 43
moon *n* 34
morning *n* 8
mother *n* 3
motorcycle *n* 25
mountain *n* 27
mouse *n* 16
mouse *n* 28
mouth *n* 40
move *v* 19
movie *n* 21
movie star *n* 21
museum *n* 33
mushroom *n* 23
music *n* 41, 52

musician *n* 41
mustache *n* 40

N

name *n* 30
neck *n* 6
necklace *n* 48
nest *n* 47
net *n* 29
new *adj* 25
newspaper *n* 46
next to *prep* 12
nice *adj* 9
night *n* 8
nine *num* 2
nineteen *num* 4
ninety *num* **p216**
ninety-eight *num* **p216**
ninety-five *num* **p216**
ninety-four *num* **p216**
ninety-nine *num* **p216**
ninety-one *num* **p216**
ninety-seven *num* **p216**
ninety-six *num* **p216**
ninety-three *num* **p216**
ninety-two *num* **p216**
noisy *adj* 47
noodles *n* 7
north *n* 48
nose *n* 11
notepad *n* 45
November *n* **p217**
numbers *n* 2
nurse *n* 18

O

ocean *n* 15
October *n* **p217**
octopus *n* 20
office *n* 31
old *adj* 9, 25
olives *n* 38
on *prep* 12
one *num* 1
one hundred *num* **p216**
one million *num* **p216**
one thousand *num* **p216**

onion *n* 23
open *v* 8
orange *n* 1
orange *n* 4
order *v* 37
outside *prep* 28
oven *n* 31
over *prep* 28
owl *n* 46

P

paint *n* 2
paint *v* 44
painting *n* 14
pajamas *n* 7
pan *n* 52
pancake *n* 12
panda *n* 26
pants *n* 11
paper *n* 2
parent *n* 18
park *n* 3
parking lot *n* 45
parrot *n* 26
party *n* 16
pasta *n* 14
path *n* 34
pattern *n* 50
paw *n* 49
pay *v* 37
peach *n* 20
pear *n* 5
peas *n* 15
pen *n* 2
pencil *n* 2
penguin *n* 37
people *n* 10
pepper *n* 15
pepper *n* 52
perfume *n* 37
person *n* 10
pets *n* 6
phone *v* 24
photo *n* 34
photographer *n* 48
pick up *v* 8
picnic *n* 34

picture *n* 27
pie *n* 29
pig *n* 19
pilot *n* 38
pineapple *n* 1
pink *n* 4
pizza *n* 7
planet *n* 48
plant *n* 13
plant *v* 41
plastic *n* 49
plate *n* 33
platform *n* 39
play *v* 15, 32
play the guitar *v* 11
play the piano *v* 11
player *n* 39
playground *n* 3
plumber *n* 50
pocket *n* 51
point *v* 5
polar bear *n* 37
police officer *n* 18
polka dots *n* 50
pond *n* 37
pool *n* 41
pop star *n* 41
post office *n* 21
postcard *n* 34
poster *n* 8
pot *n* 52
potato *n* 15
practice *v* 22
prepare *v* 37
present *n* 19
pretty *adj* 9
prince *n* 51
princess *n* 51
printer *n* 28
prize *n* 50
project *n* 27
pull *v* 50
puppet *n* 2
puppy *n* 16
purple *n* 1
purse *n* 33, 48
push *v* 50
put on *v* 17
puzzle *n* 27

puzzle book n 46
pyramid n 24

Q

quarter n 41
queen n 51
question n 22
quiet adj 47

R

rabbit n 6
race n 36
race v 33
radio n 24
railcar n 39
railroad track n 39
rain n 13
rainbow n 13
read v 35
receptionist n 50
rectangle n 17
red adj 38
red n 1
refrigerator n 31
reindeer n 37
relax v 22
remote control n 24
repair v 51
restaurant n 32
rhino n 26
rice n 29
ride n 28
ride a bike v 20
right adj 40
ring n 48
river n 23
road n 32
robot n 10
rock n 31
rocket n 34
rocks n 46
roller skates n 15
roof n 14
rug n 7
ruler n 5
run v 13, 15

S

sad adj 12
sail v 18
salad n 38
salt n 52
same adj 25
sand n 15
sandals n 9
sandcastle n 43
sandwich n 13
Saturday n p217
sauce n 14
sausage n 12
scared adj 27
scarf n 26
scary adj 9
school n 3
science n 44
scissors n 5
score n 39
score v 20
screen n 28
sea n 6
seagull n 6
seal n 37
search v 29, 35
seasons n 42
seat n 21
seaweed n 46
second adj 50
see v 52
seesaw n 21
sell v 43
send v 24
sentence n 22
September n p217
seven num 2
seventeen num 4
seventy num p216
shapes n 17
shark n 20
shed n 14
sheep n 4
shelf n 26
shell n 46
ship n 6
shirt n 11
shoes n 9
shop v 17

shopping n 33
shopping center n 45
short adj 18
shorts n 9
shoulder n 20
shout v 24
shovel n 43
show v 34
shower n 26
sick adj 39
silver n 36
sing v 11
singer n 43
sink n 27
sister n 14
sit down v 8
six num 2
sixteen num 4
sixty num p216
skate v 20
skateboard n 10
skateboard v 20
ski v 20
skiing n 47
skip v 15
skirt n 11
skis n 36
sky n 31
skyscraper n 33
sled n 36
sledding n 47
sleep v 45
slide n 21
slow adj 44
small adj 11
smell v 52
smile n 29
smoke n 42
snack n 13
snail n 39
snake n 24
sneakers n 15
snow n 32
snowball n 32
snowboard n 36
snowboarding n 47
snowflake n 32
snowman n 32
soap n 27

soccer n 23
socks n 7
soft adj 51
son n 3
sore adj 39
soup n 29
south n 48
space n 48
speak v 34
speakers n 24
spell v 3
spider n 39
spoon n 49
sports n 14
sports center n 35
spring n 42
square n 17
squirrel n 46
stable n 19
stadium n 31
stage n 43
stairs n 22
stamp n 30
stand up v 8
starfish n 46
stars n 48
start v 33
station n 39
step n 25
stomach n 23
stomachache n 30
stone n 49
stores n 45
storm n 13
story n 27
stove n 31
straight adj 18
strawberry n 20
stream n 34
street n 3
stripes n 50
strong adj 51
student n 45
study v 35
subjects n 47
sugar n 36
suitcase n 38
summer n 42
sun n 34

Sunday n p217
sunglasses n 41
sunny adj 28
supermarket n 31
surf v 18
surprised adj 12
swan n 37
sweater n 26
swim v 18
swimming n 22
swimming pool n 22
swimsuit n 22
swing n 21
swing v 32

T

table n 19
table tennis n 23
tablet n 21
tail n 49
take a photo v 11
take off v 36
talk v 24
tall adj 35
taste v 52
taxi n 24
tea n 36
teach v 5
teacher n 1
team n 39
teddy bear n 2
teeth n 29
telephone n 16
telescope n 48
television n 7
tell v 26
ten num 2, p216
tennis n 6
tennis racket n 15
tent n 42
theater n 21, 43
thin adj 44
think v 49
third adj 50
thirsty adj 27
thirteen num 3
thirty num p216
three num 1

throw v 9
Thursday n p217
ticket n 21
tidy adj 47
tidy v 22
tie n 51
tiger n 8
timetable n 44
tire n 52
tired adj 39
toes n 23
toilet n 26
tomato n 38
tongue n 29
toolbox n 42
tools n 42
tooth n 29
toothbrush n 27
toothpaste n 27
top adj 35
tortoise n 23
touch v 19
tour n 34
towel n 22
town n 21
toy box n 8
toy store n 21
toys n 8
tractor n 10
traffic n 32
traffic lights n 32
trailer n 42
train n 39
trash can n 31
travel v 34
tree n 13
triangle n 17
truck n 25
try v 29
T-shirt n 9
Tuesday n p217
turn v 32
turn off v 51
turn on v 51
TV n 24
twelve num 3
twenty num 4, p216
two num 1

U

uncle n 14
under prep 28
underwear n 7
untidy adj 47
upstairs n 22

V

vacation n 38
vegetables n 15
vet n 18
video v 33
video game n 10
view n 34
village n 30
violin n 52
visit v 38
volleyball n 23

W

wait v 17
waiter n 32
wake up v 25
walk v 13, 19
wall n 25
walrus n 37
warm adj 35
wash v 16
watch n 48
watch v 33
water n 17
water v 41
waterfall n 23
watermelon n 5
wave n 15
wave v 19
weak adj 51
weather n 28
website n 31
Wednesday n p217
week n 43
weekend n 43
weigh v 43
west n 48
wet adj 35
whale n 20
wheel n 52

whiskers n 49
whisper v 35
whistle v 32
white n 4
whole n 41
wind n 13
window n 30
windy adj 28
wing n 47
winner n 36
winter n 42
wolf n 46
woman n 7
women n 10
wood n 49
woods n 30
wool n 49
words n 1
work v 34
write v 3

X

X-ray n 45

Y

yard n 14
year n 43
yellow n 1
yogurt n 13
young adj 9

Z

zebra n 5
zero num p216
zipper n 51
zoo n 33

German word list

Each word is followed by the number of the week it appears in. For words that are not in a weekly unit, a page number is given (for example, **p216**).

In German, all nouns (things or people) are either masculine, feminine, or neuter (see p6). Adjectives (describing words) also change depending on the gender of the noun they are describing. When two options for nouns or adjectives are given in the following list (for example, der Designer / die Designerin), the masculine is given before the feminine. Where three translations are given, the masculine appears first, followed by the feminine, and then the neuter.

All nouns start with a capital letter in German. Most pronouns (words like I, he, she, and they) and most adjectives start with lower-case letters.

KEY

adj	adjective
n	noun
num	number
prep	preposition
v	verb

A

der Abend *n* 8
das Abendessen *n* 14
abhaken *v* 10
abheben *v* 36
die Ablage *n* 26
abschließen *v* 29
abtrocknen *v* 16
abwaschen *v* 16, 41
acht *num* 2
achtundneunzig *num* **p216**
achtzehn *num* 4
achtzig *num* **p216**
die Actionfigur *n* 2
addieren *v* 10
der Adler *n* 47
die Adresse *n* 30
der Affe *n* 8
das Alphabet *n* 2
alt *adj* 9, 25
die Ameise *n* 17
die Ampel *n* 32
die Ananas *n* 1
anders *adj* 25
die Angel *n* 29
angsteinflößend *adj* 9
ängstlich *adj* 12
ankommen *v* 38
ankreuzen *v* 10
anpflanzen *v* 41
anrufen *v* 24
ansehen *v* 33
antworten *v* 5
anziehen *v* 17
der Apfel *n* 1
die Apps *n* 21
der April *n* **p217**
arbeiten *v* 34
der Arm *n* 6
das Armband *n* 48

die Armbanduhr *n* 48
der Arzt / die Ärztin *n* 18
der Ast *n* 13
der Astronaut / die Astronautin *n* 34
die Aubergine *n* 23
auf *prep* 12
aufgeregt *adj* 27
aufklappen *v* 8
aufnehmen *v* 8
aufräumen *v* 22
aufstehen *v* 8
aufwachen *v* 25
der Aufzug *n* 12
das Auge *n* 11
die Augenbraue *n* 40
der August *n* **p217**
der Ausgang *n* 45
ausmalen *v* 3
ausschalten *v* 51
außen *prep* 28
die Aussicht *n* 34
aussteigen *v* 36
aussuchen *v* 17
das Auto *n* 25

B

das Baby *n* 7
der Bach *n* 34
der Backofen *n* 31
der Badeanzug *n* 22
die Badewanne *n* 26
das Badezimmer *n* 4
Badminton *n* 6
der Bahnhof *n* 39
der Bahnsteig *n* 39
der Balkon *n* 12
der Ball *n* 6
der Ballon *n* 16
die Banane *n* 1
die Band *n* 41
die Bank *n* 21
die Bank *n* 35
der Bär *n* 8
der Bart *n* 40

Baseball *n* 6
Basketball *n* 6
der Bauch *n* 23
die Bauchschmerzen *n* 30
bauen *v* 44
der Bauer / die Bäuerin *n* 19
der Bauernhof *n* 10
der Baum *n* 13
beenden *v* 33
begrüßen *v* 38
das Bein *n* 6
das belegte Brot *n* 13
der Berg *n* 27
die Berufe *n* 48
berühren *v* 19
bestellen *v* 37
besuchen *v* 38
das Bett *n* 8
das Bett machen *v* 25
bewölkt *adj* 28
die Bibliothek *n* 31
die Biene *n* 17
das Bild *n* 27
der Bildschirm *n* 28
billig *adj* 50
die Birne *n* 5
das Blatt *n* 13
blau *adj* 1
der Bleistift *n* 2
blond *adj* 38
die Blume *n* 13
der Boden *n* 30, 31
die Bohnen *n* 29
das Boot *n* 27
braun *adj* 4
braunhaarig *adj* 38
brennen *v* 45
das Brettspiel *n* 2
der Brief *n* 30
die Briefmarke *n* 30
die Brille *n* 37
Bronze *n* 36
das Brot *n* 14
die Brücke *n* 34
der Bruder *n* 14

die Brust *n* 20
das Buch *n* 5
das Bücherregal *n* 7
der Buchladen *n* 21
die Buchstaben *n* 2
buchstabieren *v* 3
die Bühne *n* 43
die Burg *n* 27
das Büro *n* 31
die Bürste *n* 37
der Bus *n* 24
der Busbahnhof *n* 24
die Bushaltestelle *n* 32
den Bus nehmen *v* 13
die Butter *n* 44

C

das Café *n* 21
campen *v* 45
der Cartoon *n* 46
der Clown *n* 28
das Comicbuch *n* 46
der Computer *n* 28
die Cousine *n* 14

D

das Dach *n* 14
das Datum *n* 22
die Decke *n* 30
die Decke *n* 34
der Delfin *n* 20
der Designer / die Designerin *n* 48
Deutsch *n* 44
der Dezember *n* **p217**
dick *adj* 44
der Dienstag *n* **p217**
der Dinosaurier *n* 10
der Donnerstag *n* **p217**
das Dorf *n* 30
der Drachen *n* 6
drehen *v* 32
drei *num* 1
das Dreieck *n* 17

dreißig *num* **p216**
dreiundneunzig *num* **p216**
dreizehn *num* 3
dritter Platz *n* 50
der Drucker *n* 28
der Dschungel *n* 8
dunkel *adj* 40
dünn *adj* 44
durstig *adj* 27
die Dusche *n* 26
die DVD *n* 24

E

das E-Book *n* 21
die Ecke *n* 41
das Ei *n* 12
das Eichhörnchen *n* 46
die Eidechse *n* 23
der Eimer *n* 43
der Eingang *n* 45
der Einkauf *n* 33
einkaufen *v* 17
der Einkaufswagen *n* 33
das Einkaufszentrum *n* 45
einkreisen *v* 10
die Einladung *n* 16
eins *num* 1
einschalten *v* 51
einsteigen *v* 36
die Eintrittskarte *n* 21
einundneunzig *num* **p216**
das Eis *n* 28
das Eis *n* 32
der Eisbär *n* 37
Eishockey *n* 47
der Elefant *n* 5
elf *num* 3
der Ellbogen *n* 20
der Elternteil *n* 18
die E-Mail *n* 21
der Enkel *n* 9
die Enkelin *n* 9
entdecken *v* 49
die Ente *n* 37

entwerfen *v* 49
die Erbsen *n* 15
die Erdbeere *n* 20
die Erde *n* 34
das Erdgeschoss *n* 12
Erdkunde *n* 47
erfinden *v* 49
die Erkältung *n* 30
erster Platz *n* 50
der Erwachsene / die Erwachsene *n* 18
erzählen *v* 26
der Esel *n* 19
essen *v* 16
das Essen *n* 32
die Essstäbchen *n* 49
das Esszimmer *n* 4
die Eule *n* 46

F

die Fabrik *n* 35
die Fächer *n* 47
die Fahne *n* 43
fahren *v* 13
der Fahrer *n* 24
der Fahrgast *n* 24
das Fahrgeschäft *n* 28
das Fahrrad *n* 21
Fahrrad fahren *v* 20
fallen lassen *v* 50
falsch *adj* 22
die Familie *n* 3
fangen *v* 9
die Farbe *n* 2
die Farben *n* 1
der Februar *n* **p217**
die Feier *n* 16
das Feld *n* 10
das Fell *n* 49
die Felsen *n* 46
das Fenster *n* 30
die Fernbedienung *n* 24
der Fernseher *n* 7, 24
festhalten *v* 50
das Festival *n* 41

das Feuer *n* 42
die Feuerwehr *n* 35
das Feuerwehrauto *n* 25
der Feuerwehrmann / die Feuerwehrfrau *n* 18
der Film *n* 21
filmen *v* 33
der Filmstar *n* 21
finden *v* 29
die Finger *n* 20
der Fisch *n* 29
fischen *v* 18
das Fischen *n* 29
das Fitnessstudio *n* 31
die Flasche *n* 33
flauschig *adj* 44
das Fleisch *n* 29
die Fleischklößchen *n* 14
die Fliege *n* 39
fliegen *v* 18
der Flügel *n* 47
der Flughafen *n* 38
das Flugzeug *n* 38
der Flur *n* 22
der Fluss *n* 23
flüstern *v* 35
die Formen *n* 17
das Foto *n* 34
der Fotoapparat *n* 34
der Fotograf / die Fotografin *n* 48
ein Foto machen *v* 11
die Frage *n* 22
fragen *v* 17
die Frau *n* 7
die Frauen *n* 10
der Freitag *n* **p217**
Fremdsprachen *n* 47
die Freunde *n* 18
freundlich *adj* 27
der Frisör / die Frisörin *n* 50
fröhlich *adj* 12
der Frosch *n* 8, 37
der Frühling *n* 42
das Frühstück *n* 12

der Fuchs *n* **46**
fühlen *v* **52**
die Führung *n* **34**
der Füller *n* **2**
fünf *num* **1**
fünfundneunzig *num* **p216**
fünfzehn *num* **3**
fünfzig *num* **p216**
der Fuß *n* **23**
Fußball **23**
die Fußmatte *n* **25**
füttern *v* **40**

G

die Gabel *n* **49**
ganz *adj* **41**
der Garten *n* **14**
geben *v* **38, 43**
die Geburtstagsfeier *n* **19**
gehen *v* **19**
die Geige *n* **52**
gelangweilt *adj* **47**
gelb *adj* **1**
das Geld *n* **33**
der Geldbeutel *n* **33**
das Gemüse *n* **15**
das Geschenk *n* **19**
die Geschichte *n* **27**
Geschichte *n* **47**
das Gesicht *n* **11**
die Getränke *n* **17**
der Gewinner *n* **36**
gießen *v* **41**
die Giraffe *n* **5**
Gitarre spielen *v* **11**
das Glas *n* **33**
glatt *adj* **18**
gleich *adj* **25**
Gold *n* **36**
der Goldfisch *n* **6**
Golf *n* **23**
der Gorilla *n* **26**
das Gras *n* **37**
grauhaarig *adj* **38**
groß *adj* **11, 35**

die Großeltern *n* **9**
die Großmutter *n* **9**
der Großvater *n* **9**
grün *adj* **1**
die Gruppe *n* **18**
der Gürtel *n* **51**

H

das Haar *n* **18**
der Hai *n* **20**
halb *adj* **46**
die Hälfte *n* **41**
der Hals *n* **6**
das Halsband *n* **49**
die Halskette *n* **48**
der Hamburger *n* **7**
die Hand *n* **20**
die Handschuhe *n* **26**
die Handtasche *n* **48**
das Handtuch *n* **22**
das Handy *n* **31**
hart *adj* **51**
das Haus *n* **3**
Hausaufgaben machen *v* **22**
die Haustiere *n* **6**
heiß *adj* **35**
helfen *v* **26**
hell *adj* **40**
der Helm *n* **15**
das Hemd *n* **11**
der Herbst *n* **42**
der Herd *n* **31**
der Himmel *n* **31**
hinsetzen *v* **8**
hinten *adj* **40**
hinter *prep* **12**
der Hirsch *n* **46**
die Hobbys *n* **14**
hochheben *v* **50**
Hockey *n* **6**
der Hockeyschläger *n* **36**
die Höhle *n* **23**
holen *v* **40**
das Holz *n* **49**
der Honig *n* **44**

hören *v* **52**
die Hose *n* **11**
das Hotel *n* **41**
hübsch *adj* **9**
die Hügel *n* **30**
das Huhn *n* **4**
das Hühnchen *n* **7**
der Hund *n* **6, 16**
hundert *num* **p216**
hungrig *adj* **27**
hüpfen *v* **32**
der Husten *n* **30**
der Hut *n* **41**
die Hütte *n* **14**

I

in *prep* **12**
in der Mitte *adj* **35**
innen *prep* **28**
die Insekten *n* **31**
die Insel *n* **15**
die Instrumente *n* **52**
die Internetseite *n* **31**

J

die Jacke *n* **11**
das Jahr *n* **43**
die Jahreszeiten *n* **42**
der Jahrmarkt *n* **28**
der Januar *n* **p217**
die Jeans *n* **7**
der Joghurt *n* **13**
der Journalist /
    die Journalistin *n* **48**
der Juli *n* **p217**
jung *adj* **9**
der Junge *n* **7**
der Juni *n* **p217**

K

der Käfer *n* **39**
der Kaffee *n* **36**
der Kalender *n* **8, 43**
kalt *adj* **35**

das Kamel *n* **24**
der Kamm *n* **37**
das Känguru *n* **26**
das Kaninchen *n* **6**
die Kappe *n* **11**
kaputt *adj* **51**
kaputt machen *v* **40**
die Karotte *n* **15**
die Karte *n* **19**
die Kartoffel *n* **15**
der Käse *n* **38**
das Kätzchen *n* **16**
die Katze *n* **6, 16**
kaufen *v* **43**
der Keks *n* **36**
der Keller *n* **22**
der Kellner / die Kellnerin *n* **32**
die Kerze *n* **19**
kicken *v* **9**
das Kind *n* **18**
die Kinder *n* **10**
das Kinn *n* **40**
das Kino *n* **21**
die Kirsche *n* **20**
das Kissen *n* **19**
die Kiste *n* **52**
die Kiwi *n* **5**
der Klassenkamerad /
    die Klassenkameradin *n* **2**
das Klassenzimmer *n* **2**
klatschen *v* **19**
die Klaue *n* **47**
Klavier spielen *v* **11**
kleben *v* **44**
der Klebstoff *n* **42**
das Kleid *n* **9**
die Kleidung *n* **7**
klein *adj* **11, 35**
die Kleinstadt *n* **21**
der Klempner /
    die Klempnerin *n* **50**
klettern *v* **15**
das Knie *n* **23**
der Knoblauch *n* **23**
der Knopf *n* **51**

kochen v 16
der Koch / die Köchin n 32
der Koffer n 38
der Kohl n 23
die Kokosnuss n 5
der Komet n 48
der Kompass n 48
der König n 51
die Königin n 51
das Konzert n 52
der Kopf n 6
die Kopfhörer n 31
der Kopfsalat n 38
die Kopfschmerzen n 30
der Korb n 33
der Körper n 6
die Krabbe n 46
krank adj 39
das Krankenhaus n 35
der Krankenpfleger /
   die Krankenpflegerin n 18
der Krankenwagen n 25
die Krawatte n 51
der Kreis n 17
das Krokodil n 24
die Krone n 51
die Küche n 4
der Kuchen n 19
die Kuh n 4
der Kühlschrank n 31
der Kuli n 2
Kunst n 44
der Künstler / die Künstlerin n
   48
der Kunststoff n 49
kurz adj 18
die kurzen Hosen n 9

L

das Lächeln n 29
lachen v 45
das Ladegerät n 31
die Läden n 45
die Lampe n 16
das Land n 30

landen v 36
die Landkarte n 45
lang adj 18
langsam adj 44
der Laptop n 31
der Lastwagen n 25
laufen v 13, 15
laut adj 40, 47
die Lautsprecher n 24
leer adj 46
der Lehrer / die Lehrerin n 1
leihen v 35
die Leiter n 25
lernen v 5, 35
lesen v 35
die Leuchte n 19
die Libelle n 17
Lieblings- adj 25
lila adj 1
die Limette n 20
die Limonade n 17
das Lineal n 5
links adj 40
die Lippen n 11
lockig adj 18
der Löffel n 49
der Löwe n 5

M

das Mädchen n 7
das Magazin n 46
die Mahlzeit n 49
der Mai n p217
mailen v 24
das Malen n 14
malen v 44
die Mango n 5
der Mann n 7
die Männer n 10
die Mannschaft n 39
der Mantel n 26
der Marienkäfer n 17
die Marionette n 2
der Markt n 30
die Marmelade n 44

der März n p217
die Maschine n 42
die Maske n 45
Mathe n 44
die Mauer n 25
die Maus n 16
die Maus n 28
der Mechaniker /
   die Mechanikerin n 52
die Medizin n 45
das Meer n 6
das Mehl n 44
die Menschen n 10
das Messer n 49
das Metall n 49
das Mietshaus n 12
die Mikrowelle n 52
die Milch n 36
der Milchshake n 17
eine Million num p216
die Minute n 42
mischen v 44
mitbringen v 38
Mittag n 42
das Mittagessen n 13
die Mitte n 41
Mitternacht n 42
der Mittwoch n p217
mögen v 37
der Monat n 43
der Mond n 34
das Monster n 10
der Montag n p217
der Morgen n 8
der Motor n 52
das Motorrad n 25
die Möwe n 6
müde adj 39
der Mülleimer n 31
der Mund n 40
die Muschel n 46
das Museum n 33
die Musik n 41, 52

der Musiker / die Musikerin n
   41
das Müsli n 12
das Muster n 50
mutig adj 39
die Mutter n 3

N

nachdenken v 49
der Nachmittag n 8
die Nachricht n 21
die Nacht n 8
der Name n 30
die Nase n 11
das Nashorn n 26
nass adj 35
Naturwissenschaften n 44
der Nebel n 13
neben prep 12
neblig adj 28
das Nest n 47
nett adj 9
das Netz n 29
neu adj 25
neun num 2
neunundneunzig num p216
neunzehn num 4
neunzig num p216
nicht mögen v 37
das Nilpferd n 5
der Norden n 48
das Notizbuch n 45
der November n p217
die Nudeln n 7
die Nudeln n 14
null num p216

O

oben adj 22, 35
das Obst n 13
das Ohr n 11
die Ohrenschmerzen n 30
der Oktober n p217
die Oliven n 38
der Onkel n 14

die Orange n 1
orange adj 4
ordentlich adj 47
der Osten n 48
der Ozean n 15

P

der Panda n 26
der Papagei n 26
das Papier n 2
die Paprika n 15
das Parfüm n 37
der Park n 3
der Parkplatz n 45
die Pastete n 29
die Person n 10
die Pfanne n 52
der Pfannkuchen n 12
der Pfeffer n 52
pfeifen v 32
das Pferd n 4
der Pfirsich n 20
die Pflanze n 13
das Pflaster n 45
die Pfote n 49
das Picknick n 34
der Pilot / die Pilotin n 38
der Pilz n 23
der Pinguin n 37
die Pizza n 7
das Plakat n 8
der Planet n 48
der Polizist / die Polizistin n 18
die Pommes frites n 7
der Pool n 41
der Popstar n 41
die Post n 21
der Postbote / die Postbotin n 50
die Postkarte n 34
der Preis n 50
prellen v 9
der Prinz n 51
die Prinzessin n 51
das Projekt n 27

der Pullover n 26
Punkte n 50
die Puppe n 2
das Puzzle n 27
die Pyramide n 24

Q

das Quadrat n 17
die Qualle n 20

R

das Rad n 52
Rad fahren v 13
der Radiergummi n 5
das Radio n 24
die Rakete n 34
das Rätselbuch n 46
der Rauch n 42
die Raupe n 17
das Rechteck n 17
rechts adj 40
reden v 24
der Regen n 13
der Regenbogen n 13
der Reifen n 52
die Reinigungskraft n 50
der Reis n 29
reisen v 34
der Reißverschluss n 51
das Rennen n 36
das Rentier n 37
reparieren v 44, 51
das Restaurant n 32
der Rezeptionist / die Rezeptionistin n 50
richtig adj 22
riechen v 52
der Ring n 48
die Robbe n 37
der Roboter n 10
der Rock n 11
die Rollschuhe n 15
das Röntgenbild n 45
rosa adj 4

rot adj 1
rothaarig adj 38
der Rücken n 23
der Rucksack n 5
rufen v 24
ruhig adj 47
die Rutsche n 21

S

der Saft n 17
der Salat n 38
das Salz n 52
sammeln v 41
der Samstag n p217
der Sand n 15
die Sandalen n 9
die Sandburg n 43
der Sänger / die Sängerin n 43
der Satz n 22
sauber adj 11
saubermachen v 22
Schach n 45
das Schaf n 4
der Schal n 26
die Schaufel n 43
die Schaukel n 21
schaukeln v 32
schauspielen v 49
der Schauspieler / die Schauspielerin n 43
die Schere n 5
die Scheune n 10
schicken v 24
schieben v 50
die Schiene n 39
das Schiff n 6
die Schildkröte n 23
der Schlafanzug n 7
schlafen v 45
das Schlafzimmer n 4
der Schläger n 15
die Schlange n 24
der Schlitten n 36

das Schlittenfahren n 47
Schlittschuh laufen v 20
die Schlittschuhe n 36
das Schlittschuhlaufen n 47
der Schlüssel n 30
schmecken v 52
der Schmetterling n 39
der Schmuck n 37
schmutzig adj 11
der Schnabel n 47
die Schnecke n 39
der Schnee n 32
der Schneeball n 32
die Schneeflocke n 32
der Schneemann n 32
schnell adj 44
der Schnurrbart n 40
die Schnurrhaare n 49
die Schokolade n 44
schön adj 11
der Schrank n 31
schreiben v 3
der Schreibtisch n 16
die Schuhe n 9
die Schule n 3
die Schulter n 20
der Schuss n 39
die Schüssel n 33
schwach adj 51
der Schwan n 37
der Schwanz n 49
schwarz adj 4
schwarzhaarig adj 38
das Schwein n 19
die Schwester n 14
das Schwimmbecken n 22
die Schwimmbrille n 22
schwimmen v 18
das Schwimmen n 22
die Schwimmweste n 29
sechs num 2
sechsundneunzig num p216
sechzehn num 4
sechzig num p216
der See n 27

das Seegras n 46
der Seestern n 46
segeln v 18
sehen v 52
die Seife n 27
seilspringen v 15
der September n p217
der Sessel n 7
sich anziehen v 25
sich beeilen v 36
sich bewegen v 19
sich entspannen v 22
sich kümmern v 40
sich unterhalten v 45
sich wehtun v 26
sieben num 2
siebenundneunzig num p216
siebzehn num 4
siebzig num p216
Silber n 36
singen v 11
der Sitz n 21
das Skateboard n 10
Skateboard fahren v 20
die Skier n 36
Ski fahren v 20
das Skifahren n 47
der Snack n 13
das Snowboard n 36
das Snowboardfahren n 47
die Socken n 7
das Sofa n 7
der Sohn n 3
der Sommer n 42
die Sonne n 34
die Sonnenbrille n 41
die Sonnenliege n 41
sonnig adj 28
der Sonntag n p217
die Soße n 14
die Speisekarte n 32
der Spiegel n 26
das Spiel n 16
das Spiel n 39
spielen v 15, 32

der Spieler n 39
der Spielplatz n 3
der Spielstand n 39
das Spielzeug n 8
die Spielzeugkiste n 8
der Spielzeugladen n 21
die Spinne n 39
der Sport n 14
das Sportzentrum n 35
sprechen v 34
springen v 15
das Stadion n 31
die Stadt n 33
der Stall n 19
stark adj 51
starten v 33
der Stein n 31, 49
die Sterne n 48
die Stiefel n 26
der Strand n 15
der Strandball n 43
die Straße n 3, 32
Streifen n 50
der Student / die Studentin n 45
die Stufe n 25
der Stuhl n 16, 19
die Stunde n 42
der Stundenplan n 44
der Sturm n 13
suchen v 29, 35, 51
der Süden n 48
der Supermarkt n 31
die Suppe n 29
surfen v 18
die Süßigkeiten n 16

T

das T-Shirt n 9
das Tablet n 21
die Tafel n 1
der Tag n 8
die Tante n 14
tanzen v 11
das Tanzen n 14

die Tasche n 51
die Taschenlampe n 42
die Tasse n 33
die Tastatur n 28
tausend num p216
das Taxi n 24
der Techniker / die Technikerin n 42
der Teddybär n 2
der Tee n 36
der Teich n 37
das Telefon n 16
das Teleskop n 48
der Teller n 33
Tennis n 6
der Tennisschläger n 15
der Teppich n 7, 19
teuer adj 50
das Theater n 43
der Tierarzt / die Tierärztin n 18
die Tiere n 10
der Tierpark n 33
der Tiger n 8
der Tintenfisch n 20
der Tisch n 19
Tischtennis n 23
die Tochter n 3
die Toilette n 26
die Tomate n 38
der Topf n 52
das Tor n 25
tragen v 43
der Traktor n 10
die Trauben n 1
träumen v 25
traurig adj 12
treffen v 9
treffen v 20
treffen v 34
die Treppe n 22
trinken v 16
trocken adj 35
die Trommel n 52
die Tür n 30

Turnen n 23
die Turnschuhe n 15

U

übel adj 39
üben v 22
über prep 28
überrascht adj 12
die Uhr n 16, 42
umfallen v 26
der Umschlag n 30
die Universität n 33
unordentlich adj 47
unten adj 35
unten n 22
unter prep 28
der Unterricht n 1, 27
unterrichten v 5
die Unterwäsche n 7
der Urlaub n 38

V

der Vater n 3
verängstigt adj 27
der Verband n 45
verkaufen v 43
der Verkehr n 32
verstecken v 40
versuchen v 29
das Videospiel n 10
viele adj 46
vier num 1
das Viertel n 41
vierundneunzig num p216
vierzehn num 3
vierzig num p216
der Vogel n 19
voll adj 46
Volleyball n 23
vor prep 12
der Vorhang n 43
vorne adj 40

W

wach *adj* 40
die Wachsmalkreide *n* 2
der Waggon *n* 39
der Wal *n* 20
der Wald *n* 27, 30
das Walross *n* 37
warm *adj* 35
warten *v* 17
das Waschbecken *n* 27
waschen *v* 16
das Wasser *n* 17
der Wasserfall *n* 23
der Wasserhahn *n* 27
die Wassermelone *n* 5
wechseln *v* 51
der Weg *n* 34
weich *adj* 51
weinen *v* 26
weiß *adj* 4
weit weg *adj* 40
die Welle *n* 15
der Welpe *n* 16
der Weltraum *n* 48
wenige *adj* 46

werfen *v* 9
Werken *n* 47
das Werkzeug *n* 42
der Werkzeugkasten *n* 42
der Westen *n* 48
der Wettbewerb *n* 50
das Wetter *n* 28
ein Wettrennen machen *v* 33
wiegen *v* 43
der Wind *n* 13
windig *adj* 28
winken *v* 19
der Winter *n* 42
die Wippe *n* 21
die Woche *n* 43
das Wochenende *n* 43
die Wohnung *n* 12
der Wohnwagen *n* 42
das Wohnzimmer *n* 4
der Wolf *n* 46
die Wolke *n* 41
der Wolkenkratzer *n* 33
die Wolle *n* 49
die Wörter *n* 1
das Wörterbuch *n* 45

wund *adj* 39
die Wurst *n* 12
die Wüste *n* 24
wütend *adj* 12

Z

die Zahlen *n* 2
zahlen *v* 37
zählen *v* 3
der Zahn *n* 29
der Zahnarzt /
   die Zahnärztin *n* 29
die Zahnbürste *n* 27
die Zähne *n* 29
die Zähne putzen *v* 25
die Zahnpasta *n* 27
der Zaun *n* 14
das Zebra *n* 5
der Zebrastreifen *n* 32
die Zehen *n* 23
zehn *num* 2, **p216**
zeichnen *v* 3
das Zeichnen *n* 14
zeigen *v* 5
zeigen *v* 34

die Zeitung *n* 46
das Zelt *n* 42
die Ziege *n* 4
ziehen *v* 50
der Zirkus *n* 28
die Zitrone *n* 20
zubereiten *v* 37
zu Fuß gehen *v* 13
der Zucker *n* 36
der Zug *n* 39
das Zuhause *n* 14
zuhören *v* 5
zuklappen *v* 8
die Zunge *n* 29
zuordnen *v* 10
zusammenfügen *v* 29
zuschneiden *v* 41
zwanzig *num* 4, **p216**
zwei *num* 1
zweiter Platz *adj* 50
zweiundneunzig *num* **p216**
die Zwiebel *n* 23
zwischen *prep* 28
zwölf *num* 3

Common subjects

This is an index of common topics found in the book. Each subject is followed by the weeks it is taught in or the page number it appears on (for example, **p216**).

animals
4, 5, 6, 8, 16, 17, 19, 20, 23, 24, 26, 37, 39, 46, 47, 49

body
6, 11, 18, 20, 23, 29, 38, 40

clothes
7, 9, 11, 15, 26, 51

directions
12, 28, 40, 48

family
3, 9, 14

feelings
12, 27

food and drink
1, 5, 7, 12, 13, 14, 15, 16, 17, 20, 23, 29, 36, 38, 44, 49, 52

health
30, 39, 45

hobbies
11, 14, 15, 18, 20, 21, 22, 29, 32, 36, 41, 43, 44, 46, 47, 49, 52

home
4, 7, 8, 12, 14, 16, 19, 22, 24, 25, 26, 27, 30, 31, 33, 37, 52

jobs
18, 29, 34, 41, 42, 43, 48, 50

nature
13, 15, 23, 24, 27, 30, 31, 37, 41, 42, 46

numbers
1, 2, 3, 4, p216

people
7, 10, 18, 51

places
3, 10, 21, 24, 27, 28, 30, 31, 32, 33, 34, 35, 45

school
1, 2, 3, 5, 8, 10, 22, 27, 35, 44, 45, 47

shapes and colors
1, 4, 17

space
34, 48

sports
6, 9, 15, 20, 22, 23, 33, 36, 39, 47, 50

technology
21, 24, 28, 31, 42

time
8, 42, 43, p217

toys
2, 8, 10

transport
13, 24, 25, 32, 36, 38, 39, 52

vacations
6, 11, 15, 34, 38, 41, 42, 43, 45

weather
13, 28, 32, 35

Answers

Week 1

1
1. der Lehrer
2. die Tafel
3. die Farben
4. die Wörter
5. der Unterricht

2
1. lila
2. rot
3. gelb
4. blau
5. grün

3
1. zwei
2. fünf
3. vier
4. eins
5. drei

4
1. die Ananas
2. die Trauben
3. der Apfel
4. die Banane
5. die Orange

Week 2

1
1. die Zahlen
2. das Alphabet
3. die Buchstaben
4. die Klassenkameradin
5. das Klassenzimmer

2
1. die Puppe
2. die Actionfigur
3. der Teddybär
4. das Brettspiel
5. die Marionette

3
1. B 2. A 3. B 4. A
5. A

4
1. acht
2. sechs
3. neun
4. sieben
5. zehn

Week 3

1
1. zeichnen
2. ausmalen
3. zählen
4. buchstabieren
5. schreiben

2
1. die Schule
2. der Spielplatz
3. der Park
4. die Straße
5. das Haus

3
1. elf
2. dreizehn
3. fünfzehn
4. vierzehn
5. zwölf

4
1. die Familie
2. der Vater
3. die Mutter
4. der Sohn
5. die Tochter

Week 4

1
1. braun
2. rosa
3. orange
4. weiß
5. schwarz

2
1. B 2. A 3. B 4. A
5. A

3
1. das Huhn
2. die Ziege
3. das Schaf
4. die Kuh
5. das Pferd

4
1. siebzehn
2. zwanzig
3. achtzehn
4. sechzehn
5. neunzehn

Week 5

1
1. das Zebra
2. das Nilpferd
3. der Löwe
4. die Giraffe
5. der Elefant

2
1. die Schere
2. das Buch
3. das Lineal
4. der Radiergummi
5. der Rucksack

3
1. zuhören
2. unterrichten
3. lernen
4. zeigen
5. antworten

4
1. die Kiwi
2. die Birne
3. die Wassermelone
4. die Kokosnuss
5. die Mango

Week 6

1
1. B 2. A 3. B 4. A
5. B

2
1. der Kopf
2. das Bein
3. der Körper
4. der Arm
5. der Hals

3
1. Hockey
2. Tennis
3. Baseball
4. Basketball
5. Badminton

4
1. das Meer
2. die Möwe
3. der Drachen
4. das Schiff
5. der Ball

Week 7

1
1. das Mädchen
2. der Mann
3. der Junge
4. das Baby
5. die Frau

2
1. B　2. A　3. A　4. B
5. A

3
1. das Sofa
2. der Teppich
3. der Sessel
4. das Bücherregal
5. der Fernseher

4
1. die Pizza
2. die Nudeln
3. der Hamburger
4. die Pommes frites
5. das Hühnchen

Week 8

1
1. der Tiger
2. der Frosch
3. der Affe
4. der Dschungel
5. der Bär

2
1. A　2. B　3. A　4. A
5. B

3
1. hinsetzen
2. aufklappen
3. zuklappen
4. aufnehmen
5. aufstehen

4
1. der Nachmittag
2. die Nacht
3. der Morgen
4. der Abend
5. der Tag

Week 9

1
1. die Großeltern
2. die Großmutter
3. der Großvater
4. der Enkel
5. die Enkelin

2
1. das T-Shirt
2. das Kleid
3. die Sandalen
4. die Schuhe
5. die kurzen Hosen

3
1. hübsch
2. alt
3. angsteinflößend
4. jung
5. nett

4
1. fangen
2. treffen
3. kicken
4. werfen
5. prellen

Week 10

1
1. die Person
2. die Frauen
3. die Kinder
4. die Menschen
5. die Männer

2
1. B　2. A　3. B　4. A
5. A

3
1. der Traktor
2. das Feld
3. der Bauernhof
4. die Tiere
5. die Scheune

4
1. der Dinosaurier
2. das Skateboard
3. das Videospiel
4. der Roboter
5. das Monster

Week 11

1
1. das Auge
2. die Lippen
3. die Nase
4. das Ohr
5. das Gesicht

2
1. A　2. B　3. A　4. A
5. B

3
1. schön
2. sauber
3. klein
4. schmutzig
5. groß

4
1. das Hemd
2. die Kappe
3. der Rock
4. die Hose
5. die Jacke

Week 12

1
1. in
2. vor
3. hinter
4. neben
5. auf

2
1. das Müsli
2. das Frühstück
3. das Ei
4. der Pfannkuchen
5. die Wurst

3
1. der Balkon
2. der Aufzug
3. das Mietshaus
4. das Erdgeschoss
5. die Wohnung

4
1. überrascht
2. traurig
3. ängstlich
4. fröhlich
5. wütend

Week 13

1
1. A　2. A　3. B　4. A
5. B

2
1. das Blatt
2. der Ast
3. der Baum
4. die Pflanze
5. die Blume

3

1 der Sturm
2 der Wind
3 der Nebel
4 der Regen
5 der Regenbogen

4

1 der Snack
2 der Joghurt
3 das Obst
4 das belegte Brot
5 das Mittagessen

Week 14

1

1 das Dach
2 der Zaun
3 der Garten
4 die Hütte
5 das Zuhause

2

1 das Zeichnen
2 das Tanzen
3 das Malen
4 der Sport
5 die Hobbys

3

1 der Onkel
2 die Tante
3 die Cousine
4 der Bruder
5 die Schwester

4

1 die Nudeln
2 die Soße
3 das Abendessen
4 das Brot
5 die Fleischklößchen

Week 15

1

1 die Karotte
2 die Erbsen
3 das Gemüse
4 die Kartoffel
5 die Paprika

2

1 der Ozean
2 die Welle
3 der Strand
4 der Sand
5 die Insel

3

1 der Helm
2 die Turnschuhe
3 der Schläger
4 der Tennisschläger
5 die Rollschuhe

4

1 laufen
2 seilspringen
3 spielen
4 klettern
5 springen

Week 16

1

1 die Süßigkeiten
2 die Feier
3 das Spiel
4 die Einladung
5 der Ballon

2

1 kochen
2 essen
3 abwaschen
4 abtrocknen
5 trinken

3

1 die Katze
2 die Maus
3 der Hund
4 der Welpe
5 das Kätzchen

4

1 die Lampe
2 die Uhr
3 das Telefon
4 der Schreibtisch
5 der Stuhl

Week 17

1

1 fragen
2 aussuchen
3 warten
4 anziehen
5 einkaufen

2

1 der Marienkäfer
2 die Biene
3 die Ameise
4 die Libelle
5 die Raupe

3

1 der Saft
2 die Getränke
3 das Wasser
4 die Limonade
5 der Milchshake

4

1 das Dreieck
2 der Kreis
3 das Rechteck
4 das Quadrat
5 die Formen

Week 18

1

1 A 2 B 3 B 4 A
5 B

2

1 das Haar
2 kurz
3 lang
4 glatt
5 lockig

3

1 surfen
2 fischen
3 fliegen
4 schwimmen
5 segeln

4

1 das Kind
2 die Erwachsene
3 der Elternteil
4 die Gruppe
5 die Freunde

Week 19

1

1 sich bewegen
2 gehen
3 berühren
4 klatschen
5 winken

2

1 der Vogel
2 der Esel
3 der Stall
4 das Schwein
5 der Bauer

3
1. das Geschenk
2. die Karte
3. die Geburtstagsfeier
4. die Kerze
5. der Kuchen

4
1. der Teppich
2. das Kissen
3. die Leuchte
4. der Stuhl
5. der Tisch

Week 20

1
1. A 2. B 3. A 4. B
5. A

2
1. der Delfin
2. die Qualle
3. der Tintenfisch
4. der Hai
5. der Wal

3
1. die Finger
2. die Schulter
3. der Ellbogen
4. die Hand
5. die Brust

4
1. die Zitrone
2. die Kirsche
3. die Erdbeere
4. der Pfirsich
5. die Limette

Week 21

1
1. das Tablet
2. das E-Book
3. die Nachricht
4. die Apps
5. die E-Mail

12
1. der Buchladen
2. die Post
3. der Spielzeugladen
4. das Café
5. die Kleinstadt

3
1. der Sitz
2. das Kino
3. der Filmstar
4. die Eintrittskarte
5. der Film

4
1. A 2. B 3. A 4. A
5. B

Week 22

1
1. der Flur
2. oben
3. unten
4. die Treppe
5. der Keller

2
1. Hausaufgaben machen
2. aufräumen
3. üben
4. sich entspannen
5. saubermachen

3
1. das Handtuch
2. das Schwimmbecken
3. der Badeanzug
4. die Schwimmbrille
5. das Schwimmen

4
1. richtig
2. die Frage
3. das Datum
4. falsch
5. der Satz

Week 23

1
1. die Zwiebel
2. der Knoblauch
3. der Kohl
4. der Pilz
5. die Aubergine

2
1. der Fluss
2. der Wasserfall
3. die Höhle
4. die Eidechse
5. die Schildkröte

3
1. Golf
2. Volleyball
3. Turnen
4. Tischtennis
5. Fußball

4
1. der Rücken
2. der Bauch
3. das Knie
4. der Fuß
5. die Zehen

Week 24

1
1. A 2. B 3. B 4. A
5. B

2
1. das Kamel
2. die Pyramide
3. die Wüste
4. die Schlange
5. das Krokodil

3
1. das Taxi
2. der Fahrgast
3. der Bus
4. der Fahrer
5. der Busbahnhof

4
1. anrufen
2. mailen
3. schicken
4. rufen
5. reden

Week 25

1
1. die Stufe
2. die Fußmatte
3. die Mauer
4. die Leiter
5. das Tor

2
1. das Auto
2. der Lastwagen
3. das Motorrad
4. das Feuerwehrauto
5. der Krankenwagen

3
1. B 2. A 3. A 4. B
5. A

4

1 gleich
2 anders
3 neu
4 Lieblingsteddybär
5 alt

Week 26

1

1 erzählen
2 weinen
3 helfen
4 sich wehtun
5 umfallen

2

1 das Känguru
2 der Gorilla
3 das Nashorn
4 der Panda
5 der Papagei

3

1 die Stiefel
2 der Pullover
3 der Schal
4 der Mantel
5 die Handschuhe

4

1 die Badewanne
2 die Toilette
3 der Spiegel
4 die Ablage
5 die Dusche

Week 27

1

1 verängstigt
2 aufgeregt
3 freundlich
4 durstig
5 hungrig

2

1 die Seife
2 das Waschbecken
3 die Zahnpasta
4 die Zahnbürste
5 der Wasserhahn

3

1 das Projekt
2 das Puzzle
3 das Bild
4 die Geschichte
5 der Unterricht

4

1 der Wald
2 der Berg
3 die Burg
4 der See
5 das Boot

Week 28

1

1 A 2 B 3 B 4 A
5 B

2

1 neblig
2 sonnig
3 das Wetter
4 windig
5 bewölkt

3

1 die Maus
2 der Drucker
3 der Computer
4 der Bildschirm
5 die Tastatur

4

1 der Zirkus
2 das Fahrgeschäft
3 das Eis
4 der Jahrmarkt
5 der Clown

Week 29

1

1 suchen
2 finden
3 zusammenfügen
4 abschließen
5 versuchen

2

1 der Fisch
2 das Fischen
3 die Angel
4 das Netz
5 die Schwimmweste

3

1 die Zähne
2 die Zunge
3 der Zahn
4 das Lächeln
5 die Zahnärztin

4

1 die Bohnen
2 das Fleisch
3 der Reis
4 die Suppe
5 die Pastete

Week 30

1

1 das Dorf
2 die Hügel
3 das Land
4 das Wald
5 der Markt

2

1 der Brief
2 die Adresse
3 der Umschlag
4 die Briefmarke
5 der Name

3

1 B 2 A 3 B 4 A
5 B

4

1 die Decke
2 das Fenster
3 die Tür
4 der Boden
5 der Schlüssel

Week 31

1

1 B 2 B 3 B 4 A
5 A

2

1 das Büro
2 die Bibliothek
3 das Stadion
4 das Fitnessstudio
5 der Supermarkt

3

1 der Herd
2 der Mülleimer
3 der Backofen
4 der Schrank
5 der Kühlschrank

4

1 der Stein
2 der Himmel
3 die Wolke
4 der Boden
5 die Insekten

Week 32

1

1 B 2 A 3 A 4 A
5 B

2
1. die Speisekarte
2. das Restaurant
3. die Köchin
4. das Essen
5. die Kellnerin

3
1. spielen
2. hüpfen
3. drehen
4. schaukeln
5. pfeifen

4
1. die Straße
2. die Bushaltestelle
3. der Verkehr
4. der Zebrastreifen
5. die Ampel

Week 33

1
1. der Teller
2. die Flasche
3. das Glas
4. die Schüssel
5. die Tasse

2
1. A 2. B 3. A 4. A
5. B

3
1. der Geldbeutel
2. der Einkauf
3. der Korb
4. das Geld
5. der Einkaufswagen

4
1. der Tierpark
2. die Stadt
3. das Museum
4. die Universität
5. der Wolkenkratzer

Week 34

1
1. reisen
2. arbeiten
3. sprechen
4. treffen
5. zeigen

2
1. die Astronautin
2. die Erde
3. die Sonne
4. der Mond
5. die Rakete

3
1. die Brücke
2. der Bach
3. der Weg
4. das Picknick
5. die Decke

4
1. das Foto
2. die Aussicht
3. der Fotoapparat
4. die Führung
5. die Postkarte

Week 35

1
1. B 2. A 3. A 4. A
5. B

2
1. klein
2. unten
3. in der Mitte
4. groß
5. oben

3
1. warm
2. trocken
3. nass
4. kalt
5. heiß

4
1. lernen
2. flüstern
3. suchen
4. lesen
5. leihen

Week 36

1
1. der Tee
2. der Keks
3. der Kaffee
4. die Milch
5. der Zucker

2
1. Gold
2. der Gewinner
3. Silber
4. Bronze
5. das Rennen

3
1. abheben
2. landen
3. sich beeilen
4. aussteigen
5. einsteigen

4
1. B 2. A 3. A 4. B
5. A

Week 37

1
1. mögen
2. nicht mögen
3. zahlen
4. bestellen
5. zubereiten

2
1. der Kamm
2. die Brille
3. die Bürste
4. das Parfüm
5. der Schmuck

3
1. der Pinguin
2. der Eisbär
3. die Robbe
4. das Rentier
5. das Walross

4
1. das Gras
2. der Frosch
3. der Teich
4. der Schwan
5. die Ente

Week 38

1
1. der Pilot
2. der Flughafen
3. der Urlaub
4. der Koffer
5. das Flugzeug

2
1. mitbringen
2. ankommen
3. besuchen
4. geben
5. begrüßen

3

1. braunhaarig
2. blond
3. rothaarig
4. schwarzhaarig
5. grauhaarig

4

1. der Salat
2. der Kopfsalat
3. die Tomate
4. der Käse
5. die Oliven

Week 39

1

1. das Spiel
2. der Schuss
3. die Mannschaft
4. der Spielstand
5. der Spieler

2

1. der Käfer
2. die Fliege
3. der Schmetterling
4. die Schnecke
5. die Spinne

3

1. mutig
2. übel
3. wund
4. müde
5. krank

4

1. B 2. A 3. B 4. B
5. A

Week 40

1

1. hell
2. wach
3. dunkel
4. schlafend
5. laut

2

1. verstecken
2. holen
3. füttern
4. kaputt machen
5. sich kümmern

3

1. weit weg
2. links
3. hinten
4. rechts
5. vorne

4

1. der Mund
2. das Kinn
3. die Augenbraue
4. der Schnurrbart
5. der Bart

Week 41

1

1. ganz
2. die Ecke
3. die Hälfte
4. die Mitte
5. das Viertel

2

1. der Pool
2. der Hut
3. das Hotel
4. die Sonnenliege
5. die Sonnenbrille

3

1. B 2. A 3. B 4. A
5. A

4

1. sammeln
2. anpflanzen
3. gießen
4. wachsen
5. zuschneiden

Week 42

1

1. die Uhr
2. Mittag
3. die Minute
4. Mitternacht
5. die Stunde

2

1. das Feuer
2. der Wohnwagen
3. das Zelt
4. die Taschenlampe
5. der Rauch

3

1. der Sommer
2. der Winter
3. der Herbst
4. der Frühling
5. die Jahreszeiten

4

1. der Klebstoff
2. die Technikerin
3. der Werkzeugkasten
4. das Werkzeug
5. die Maschine

Week 43

1

1. wiegen
2. kaufen
3. geben
4. verkaufen
5. tragen

2

1. der Schauspieler
2. der Vorhang
3. die Bühne
4. die Sängerin
5. das Theater

3

1. die Fahne
2. der Strandball
3. der Eimer
4. die Schaufel
5. die Sandburg

4

1. der Monat
2. die Woche
3. das Jahr
4. der Kalender
5. das Wochenende

Week 44

1

1. Kunst
2. Mathe
3. Naturwissenschaften
4. Deutsch
5. der Stundenplan

2

1. bauen
2. malen
3. mischen
4. reparieren
5. kleben

3

1. die Butter
2. die Marmelade
3. die Schokolade
4. das Mehl
5. der Honig

4

1. flauschig
2. langsam
3. dick
4. schnell
5. dünn

Week 45

1

1. der Ausgang
2. der Parkplatz
3. die Läden
4. der Eingang
5. das Einkaufszentrum

2

1. der Student
2. die Landkarte
3. Schach
4. das Wörterbuch
5. das Notizbuch

3

1. die Medizin
2. das Röntgenbild
3. der Verband
4. das Pflaster
5. die Maske

4

1. brennen
2. lachen
3. sich unterhalten
4. campen
5. schlafen

Week 46

1

1. der Wolf
2. die Eule
3. der Hirsch
4. das Eichhörnchen
5. der Fuchs

2

1. die Krabbe
2. die Muschel
3. die Felsen
4. das Seegras
5. der Seestern

3

1. voll
2. leer
3. halb
4. wenige
5. viele

4

1. A 2. B 3. B 4. B
5. A

Week 47

1

1. Erdkunde
2. Werken
3. Geschichte
4. Fremdsprachen
5. die Fächer

2

1. das Nest
2. der Schnabel
3. der Flügel
4. die Klaue
5. der Adler

3

1. laut
2. ruhig
3. unordentlich
4. ordentlich
5. gelangweilt

4

1. A 2. B 3. A 4. B
5. B

Week 48

1

1. der Kompass
2. der Norden
3. der Westen
4. der Osten
5. der Süden

2

1. die Berufe
2. die Designerin
3. der Journalist
4. die Künstlerin
5. die Fotografin

3

1. der Ring
2. das Armband
3. die Handtasche
4. die Halskette
5. die Armbanduhr

4

1. der Komet
2. der Weltraum
3. der Planet
4. die Sterne
5. das Teleskop

Week 49

1

1. B 2. A 3. B 4. A
5. B

2

1. das Metall
2. der Stein
3. das Holz
4. der Kunststoff
5. die Wolle

3

1. die Schnurrhaare
2. die Pfote
3. der Schwanz
4. das Halsband
5. das Fell

4

1. erfinden
2. nachdenken
3. entdecken
4. schauspielen
5. entwerfen

Week 50

1

1. ziehen
2. festhalten
3. schieben
4. fallen lassen
5. hochheben

2

1. Streifen
2. teuer
3. Punkte
4. das Muster
5. billig

3

1. erster Platz
2. der Wettbewerb
3. der Preis
4. zweiter Platz
5. dritter Platz

4

1. die Reinigungskraft
2. die Rezeptionistin
3. der Frisör
4. der Klempner
5. der Postbote

Week 51

1

1. wechseln
2. suchen
3. einschalten
4. ausschalten
5. reparieren

2

1. die Krawatte
2. der Knopf
3. der Reißverschluss
4. die Tasche
5. der Gürtel

3

1. stark
2. weich
3. hart
4. kaputt
5. schwach

4

1. die Prinzessin
2. der König
3. der Prinz
4. die Krone
5. die Königin

Week 52

1

1. der Pfeffer
2. das Salz
3. die Mikrowelle
4. der Topf
5. die Pfanne

2

1. die Trommel
2. die Musik
3. das Konzert
4. die Instrumente
5. die Geige

3

1. schmecken
2. riechen
3. sehen
4. hören
5. fühlen

4

1. B
2. A
3. B
4. A
5. B

Acknowledgments

The publisher would like to thank:

Adam Brackenbury for design and illustration assistance; Edwood Burn
for illustration assistance; Ankita Awasthi Tröger and Andiamo!
Language Services Ltd for proofreading; Abigail Ellis for indexing;
DB Media for audio recording and production; Christine Stroyan and
Sophie Adam for audio recording management; and Rakesh Kumar,
Priyanka Sharma, and Saloni Singh for jacket design assistance.